QUICK WIN
ECONOMICS

Answers to your top 100 economics questions

Stephen Kinsella

Published by

OAK TREE PRESS
19 Rutland Street, Cork, Ireland
www.oaktreepress.com

© 2011 Stephen Kinsella

A catalogue record of this book is
available from the British Library.

ISBN 978 1 904887 42 3 (Paperback)
ISBN 978 1 904887 59 1 (PDF)
ISBN 978 1 904887 60 7 (ePub)
ISBN 978 1 904887 61 4 (Kindle)

INTRODUCTION

QUICK WIN ECONOMICS is aimed at practical people who understand that economics is important, because economic models inform the most powerful people in the world, who make decisions based on the advice of economists. Those decisions affect the daily lives of millions of people, for better and for worse. The mistakes of economists can have serious consequences. It pays to know what they are talking about.

Economics is one of the best set of tools for thinking about current social and political issues we have. Economics is not perfect. In fact, at the time of writing, the subject is in chaos. That said, economics is the best method we have for cutting through the 'conventional wisdom—the ideas which are esteemed at any time for their acceptability', as economist JK Galbraith defined the term. Slicing through the conventional wisdom is worth any confusion getting abreast of this set of ideas might cause you.

QUICK WIN ECONOMICS will help you decode economic phenomena – for example, you'll find out exactly why a change in central bank lending rates will change your mortgage, making you richer, or poorer. You'll find out what a stock is, and what a stock market index is. You'll understand the basics of exchange rate movements, while avoiding the detail. We will look at economic questions with as little jargon as humanly possible. I promise.

Think of **QUICK WIN ECONOMICS** as midway between a Wikipedia article and a textbook. I don't have the space, and you most likely don't have the time, for a textbook, and if you do, there are other, better places you can go to look. I'll even send you there throughout the text. But for a first look at economic ideas, for the bones of them, QUICK WIN ECONOMICS will be for you.

QUICK WIN ECONOMICS is designed to let you dip in and out as you'd like, looking for answers to questions you might have, looking for clarification, or just for a place to start. Each entry is tagged by one of five subject areas:

- Economics Essentials.

- Micro-economics.
- Macro-economics.
- Economic Policy.
- Applied Economics.

Economics Essentials does exactly what it says. You'll be introduced to the basic concepts of economics quickly, shown where and why they are relevant, where they came from, what, if anything is wrong with them, and where to find out more information if you so wish.

Micro-economics looks at the individual or the household – how they make decisions to work, to save, to consume, or to invest, and where their best opportunities lie.

Macro-economics concerns the overall relationships within the economic system. Macro questions centre around how much we produce as a country, and how much (or how little) inequality there is in an economic system.

Economic Policy looks at economic questions from a more governmental perspective – what policy measures we might implement to help our economy grow if we're in bad times, and what to do if the economy needs to develop further, or be transformed in the process of development.

Applied Economics shows you where the economic concepts are applied, in what contexts, and where they fail, and where they succeed. The emphasis is on you, your life and how these concepts relate to you.

You also can use the grid system in the contents section to search for questions and answers across a range of topics:
- Theory / definitions.
- Measurement.
- Consumers / buyers.
- Business / producers / sellers.
- Government.
- Market.

- International.

And, where it's appropriate, you'll get cross-referenced answers to sources that can give you a fuller explanation, and take your reading further.

You've picked up **QUICK WIN ECONOMICS** at an exciting time in economics. All the old rules are being torn up in the wake of the 2008 / 2009 crisis. Economic literacy has never been more important. Consider it as your invitation to the party.

Stephen Kinsella
Limerick
March 2011

ACKNOWLEDGEMENTS

Thanks to my colleagues at the Kemmy Business School for the many discussions we have had on the subject of economics, and thanks to Brian O'Kane for suggesting I write this book, and whose suggestions made it better. Of course, I remain responsible for any errors.

Thanks to my wife and family for putting up with me while I write yet another book, taking me away from them, even though I am sitting at the kitchen table most of the time.

This book is dedicated to two Lily Kinsellas. One is 88 years old, the other is 88 days old. The first Lily, my grandmother, gave me my first lessons in income, saving, and consumption, but most especially, wages. The second Lily Kinsella just absorbs most of my wages. This is the best investment I can think of making.

CONTENTS

Search by theme:

Or search by topic:

Theory / definitions

Measurement

Consumers / buyers

Business / producers / sellers

Government

Market

International

using the grid overleaf.

ECONOMICS ESSENTIALS

	Theory / definitions	Measurement	Consumers / buyers	Business / producers / sellers	Government	Market	International	Page
Q1 What is economics?	✓		✓	✓	✓	✓	✓	2
Q2 What is an economic model?	✓	✓						4
Q3 What are variables – and which matter most?	✓	✓						6
Q4 What are economic indicators?	✓	✓						8
Q5 How do economists think about costs?	✓	✓				✓		10
Q6 What are the factors of production?	✓							13
Q7 What is 'rent'?	✓	✓	✓	✓				14
Q8 What is marginal analysis?	✓	✓	✓	✓	✓			16
Q9 What is opportunity cost?	✓	✓						18
Q10 What is utility?	✓	✓	✓					20
Q11 What is a price?	✓	✓	✓	✓		✓		22
Q12 Why do economists focus on the consumer?	✓		✓					24
Q13 Why do economists assume people are rational?	✓		✓	✓	✓			26
Q14 What is bounded rationality?	✓		✓					28
Q15 Why are expectations important?	✓	✓	✓					30
Q16 What is consumer surplus?	✓	✓	✓			✓		31
Q17 What is producer surplus?	✓	✓		✓		✓		32

ECONOMICS ESSENTIALS	Theory / definitions	Measurement	Consumers / buyers	Business / producers / sellers	Government	Market	International	Page
Q18 What is a deadweight loss?	☑	☑	☑	☑	☑	☑		33
Q19 What are economic incentives and why do people react to them?	☑	☑	☑			☑		35
Q20 What is the 'market'?	☑	☑	☑	☑	☑	☑		36
Q21 What is market failure?	☑		☑	☑	☑	☑		39
Q22 What is equilibrium?	☑	☑				☑		41
Q23 What are excess supply and excess demand?	☑	☑				☑		42
Q24 What are comparative statics?	☑	☑						43
Q25 What is market structure?	☑		☑	☑		☑		45
Q26 Why do monopolies matter?	☑			☑		☑		47
Q27 What is aggregate demand / supply?	☑	☑	☑	☑	☑			48
Q28 Why are the supply chains of some companies more connected than others?				☑		☑		50
Q29 What is a barrier to entry or exit?				☑		☑		51
Q30 What is game theory and how does it help to make people better off?	☑	☑						53
Q31 What is an index?		☑					☑	55
Q32 What is arbitrage?		☑				☑		57

ECONOMICS ESSENTIALS	Theory / definitions	Measurement	Consumers / buyers	Business / producers / sellers	Government	Market	International	Page
Q33 What is economic geography?	☑						☑	58
Q34 What is an economic identity?	☑	☑						60
Q35 Why do economists use graphs?		☑						61
Q36 Why do economists use equations and functions to explain their theories?	☑	☑						63
Q37 What are good sources of economic data?		☑		☑	☑			65
Q38 What is the economic definition of risk – and how does it differ from uncertainty?	☑							67
Q39 What is risk aversion?	☑							68

MICRO-ECONOMICS	Theory / definitions	Measurement	Consumers / buyers	Business / producers / sellers	Government	Market	International	Page
Q40 How does the behavioural theory of the business explain how businesses work?	☑			☑				70
Q41 How does a business decide how much to produce?		☑		☑				72

MICRO-ECONOMICS	Theory / definitions	Measurement	Consumers / buyers	Business / producers / sellers	Government	Market	International	Page
Q42 How do businesses know how much to increase prices for a product or service?		☑		☑				74
Q43 What happens to demand for gin when the price of tonic changes?	☑					☑		76
Q44 What is break-even analysis?	☑	☑		☑	☑			77
Q45 What are diminishing returns?	☑			☑				78

MACRO-ECONOMICS	Theory / definitions	Measurement	Consumers / buyers	Business / producers / sellers	Government	Market	International	Page
Q46 What are the major '-isms' in economics?	☑							82
Q47 What is the macro-economy?	☑		☑	☑	☑			84
Q48 What is an economy's capital stock? Why does it matter?	☑			☑				86
Q49 How are the parts of the economy connected together?	☑		☑	☑	☑		☑	88
Q50 What is inflation?	☑	☑						91
Q51 What is hyperinflation?	☑	☑						93

MACRO-ECONOMICS	Theory / definitions	Measurement	Consumers / buyers	Business / producers / sellers	Government	Market	International	Page
Q52 What is deflation and why is it so worrying?	☑	☑						96
Q53 How do businesses decide which projects to fund, and which ones to drop?		☑		☑				97
Q54 Why does the same amount of money buy less today than when I was a child?	☑	☑						99
Q55 What determines the exchange rate between currencies?		☑					☑	100
Q56 Why don't Big Macs cost the same in every country?		☑					☑	101
Q57 If the government devalues the currency, will this help my business?			☑	☑	☑		☑	103
Q58 Why does every country have a central bank? What does it do?					☑			105
Q59 What is an economic and monetary union?					☑		☑	106
Q60 Why are cartels banned in most countries?				☑	☑	☑		107
Q61 What is a labour market?			☑			☑		108
Q62 What is the balance of payments?		☑					☑	110
Q63 What is globalisation?							☑	112
Q64 Does free trade work?						☑	☑	113

MACRO-ECONOMICS	Theory / definitions	Measurement	Consumers / buyers	Business / producers / sellers	Government	Market	International	Page
Q65 Why does comparative advantage mean that free trade is almost always better than restricted trade?						☑	☑	115
Q66 Why do import / export tariffs matter for free trade?					☑	☑	☑	116
Q67 What is economic efficiency?	☑							117
Q68 What are government debts and why do they matter?			☑	☑	☑		☑	118
Q69 What is liquidity?	☑	☑	☑	☑	☑		☑	120
Q70 What is Gross Domestic Product?	☑	☑					☑	121
Q71 What is the GDP deflator?	☑	☑					☑	123
Q72 What is the business cycle?		☑					☑	124
Q73 How fast should an economy grow?		☑						126
Q74 What is economic development?	☑						☑	127
Q75 What is economic inequality?	☑	☑						128
Q76 What is the paradox of thrift?	☑	☑						130

ECONOMIC POLICY	Theory / definitions	Measurement	Consumers / buyers	Business / producers / sellers	Government	Market	International	Page
Q77 Why does fiscal policy matter?	☑				☑	☑		132
Q78 What is money and why is it useful?		☑	☑	☑	☑	☑		134
Q79 What is the money supply?	☑	☑						135
Q80 Can the government manage the economy through monetary policy?	☑				☑			136
Q81 What are interest rates and why do they matter?	☑	☑		☑				138
Q82 What is a bank and how does it create money?				☑				140
Q83 How does a government create money?					☑			142
Q84 Can the government ever really manage the economy?					☑			144
Q85 What is a poverty trap and how can people get out of one?		☑	☑				☑	146

APPLIED ECONOMICS	Theory / definitions	Measurement	Consumers / buyers	Business / producers / sellers	Government	Market	International	Page
Q86 Is advertising a good thing?				☑		☑		148
Q87 How would economists deal with pollution?						☑		149
Q88 What is a demographic transition and will it affect my pension, or hurt my children's chances in life?			☑			☑		150
Q89 Can an individual ever beat the market?						☑		151
Q90 Should we tax more or less?					☑			153
Q91 Could the government help the economy to recover by reducing taxes?					☑			155
Q92 Could we ever have a zero inflation economy?					☑			157
Q93 Why does increased productivity matter for an economy?		☑			☑			158
Q94 Why does everyone want to buy a house?			☑					159
Q95 Why is there unemployment and how can it be reduced?			☑			☑		161
Q96 What is the trickle-down theory?	☑					☑		163
Q97 How do organisations like the World Trade Organisation influence world trade?					☑	☑	☑	164

APPLIED ECONOMICS	Theory / definitions	Measurement	Consumers / buyers	Business / producers / sellers	Government	Market	International	Page
Q98 How do taxes impact the market?					☑	☑		166
Q99 How do reductions in Government spending affect the economy?					☑	☑		168
Q100 Why does a change in central bank lending rates affect my mortgage?			☑		☑		☑	169
Q101 How could I spend my money to have the greatest benefit on the economy as a whole?			☑			☑		170

ECONOMICS ESSENTIALS

Q1   What is economics?

Economics is the study of the reproduction of systems of social relations in exchange. Economists study the behaviour of individuals, households, businesses, governments, and countries, when they interact with one another in particular ways.

The economic system, of which you are a part, reproduces itself, year on year, by combining the natural resources of the system: people, their knowledge and skills, land, and physical capital (buildings and machinery) – the factors of production – to produce the goods, services and trained people we need to keep everyone at the same standard of living as the year before.

Today's modern, globally-integrated economic system has evolved in several stages: from feudal relationships between lords, landowners, and the peasantry, to highly-connected international marketplaces for goods and services, dominated by competition between large corporations.

Economics studies the big questions: 'Why are we rich, why are they poor?', 'Why do I choose one set of things to consume, and not another?' or 'When should I decide to start investing in a new product or business, and when should I shut that business down?'. The answers economists give shape to the world around them, and around you, because economists' advice can change government policy and so change your life.

Fundamentally, economics is the study of how and why people choose the things they choose, whether for themselves, their business, or their country (the study of 'where' people make their choices is called economic geography). However, the world is a complicated place. Economists take a small slice of the world and examine that slice closely, 'forgetting' for a moment the rest of the world in an effort to understand. Sometimes this reduction in size and complexity works, and helps us to explain a facet of human behaviour. Sometimes it does not. The stories economists tell to help them – and us – understand the complexity of the world and its patterns are called 'models'. To be useful, these stories must fit the patterns pretty well, although sometimes they don't.

See also

Q2   What is an economic model?

Models are partial representations of reality. The best example of a model is a map, a representation of the lay of the land. You would like to know how to get from point A to point B, but you do not need the details of every blade of grass in every field along the route of your journey: a map at 1:1 scale would be useless! So you use a simplified version of reality: a map. It contains roads, train lines, housing estates, and so forth – all to a scale, which makes some sacrifices in comprehensiveness in return for its usability.

Because economic models leave out the complexity of real economies, they make it easy to analyse the behaviour of these little models. And because the assumptions of the models are chosen to represent the some of the most important features of the real economy, the model's behaviour can cast some light on the behaviour of the real economy. At least, that's the theory.

Economic models would very much like to be like maps. But they aren't. Instead, economic models are:

- Descriptive: They say things like 'people prefer more to less', or 'people must choose between two alternatives'.

- Causal: They say things like 'if the average person increased their level of education by two years, on average, they could expect a 10% increase in their wages' or 'if the government increases taxes on petrol by 10%, then motorists will drive two million fewer miles this year'. There is a cause and effect component built into most economic models.

- Predictive: They try to forecast ahead for a short time, to get a sense of where the variables we are interested in might go.

However, because economic models simplify reality, focusing on a specific area closely and 'forgetting' everything else, they rarely are as accurate as a map. You should take economic models with a grain, or perhaps a barrel, of salt. Economic models are an 'apparatus of the mind', as one famous economist, JM Keynes, said. They are a technique, to help you think through an issue you might be facing, to help you draw conclusions, and to act upon those conclusions.

Economic models are not as accurate as models of, say, molecular combination in chemistry. At their hearts, models are just stories. But, to the extent that they are helpful to our understanding, they are useful.

See also

Q3 What are variables – and which matter most?

Q3   What are variables – and which matter most?

Economic models use variables, which are just characteristics that can be changed which we can measure. Economists identify two type of variable within their models:

- Exogenous: a variable not explained by the model but taken as given.
- Endogenous: a variable explained by the model.

In chemistry, an exothermic reaction is an explosion, something that gives off heat, while an endothermic reaction is an implosion, something that sucks in heat ('exo' means 'out'; 'endo' means 'in'). In economics, exogenous variables are variables that come from outside the model, and have no causal links within the model – for example, preferences are not strictly part of the supply and demand model but, when preferences change, demand changes, which affects the model from the outside. Endogenous variables, on the other hand, are causally linked, so when price changes in the supply and demand model, supply changes, and demand changes, since price and quantity are endogenous to the supply and demand model.

We use variables to see whether a change in one variable results in a change in another. For example, when your disposable income goes down, because your wages are reduced by taxation or by inflation or by an across the board wage cut (or by all three), then your consumption will drop. There is a relationship between how much you consume, and how much disposable income you might have. We can measure that relationship when things change. The relationship might be something like:

Consumption = a+b*(disposable income).

Here, the level of consumption is determined by a constant *a* (because everyone has to eat, *a* could be €100 a week, say), and another constant *b* times the level of disposable income. If *b* were, say, 0.8, then you would consume 80% of your disposable income, and save the other 20%.

In this simple model, the endogenous variable is consumption—that's the thing explained by the changes in disposable income. The exogenous variable is disposable income. The constants in the equation are *a* and *b*.

Which variables matter most? First, we are interested in employment—the number of people employed in an economy at a given time relative to the number of people *looking for work*. Next comes the interest rate, the cost of acquiring capital. When interest rates are low, it costs very little to borrow, so economic activity will be high. When interest rates are high, it costs a lot to borrow, so economic activity may be depressed. The level of economic output by a country in a given year is very important, as is the deviation from the trend of growth of economic activity.

See also
Q2   What is an economic model?
Q20   What is the 'market'?
Q50   What is inflation?
Q81   What are interest rates and why do they matter?
Q95   Why is there unemployment and how can it be reduced?

Q4   What are economic indicators?

Economists want to predict how the economy will react to changes in external economic conditions, as well as to movements in economic variables of interest, like gross domestic product (GDP) and aggregate demand, as well as unemployment, business creation and destruction, capital formation, interest rates, and many other sources of economic data.

Economists use models to predict – but those models require input, which comes from economic indicators, such as manufacturing demand, production orders or investor confidence surveys. If these indicators suggest that the economy is going to do better or worse in the future than previously expected, investors may decide to change their investing strategy, and policy-makers may enact new policies to try to counter any negative effects.

Leading indicators change *before* the rest of the economy changes. The stock market is a good example of a leading indicator. Production orders and consumer behaviour are also useful.

Lagging indicators change after the economy has changed course. Examples here include the unemployment rate, production, and certain business activities.

Economists use leading and lagging indicators to attempt to predict future financial or economic trends. Indicators are very useful, because their movements tell us about the way the economy as a whole will move in the near future.

Say you notice that inventories in manufacturing are rising. What does this mean? It might mean that sales growth is weakening, meaning fewer people are buying manufacturing goods at the moment. This may indicate that households are not spending, because of increasing unemployment and worries about the future. This might be a leading indicator that the economy is going into a slump.

See also

Q27   What is aggregate demand / supply?
Q37   What are good sources of economic data?
Q70   What is Gross Domestic Product?
Q80   Can the government manage the economy through monetary policy?
Q81   What are interest rates and why do they matter?
Q84   Can the government ever really manage the economy?
Q95   Why is there unemployment and how can it be reduced?

Q5   How do economists think about costs?

There are many definitions and types of cost used in economics. The economic notion of cost is based on the price of inputs that a business must pay for producing a good – that is, its accounting cost, plus the opportunity cost of choosing to produce that good as opposed to another product using the same resources and factors of production.

Economists distinguish variable costs from fixed costs. Variable costs include payments to and for workers, materials, and utilities – anything that varies directly with the volume of output. So, for a hot dog seller, each extra hot dog sold requires an extra sausage and an extra bread roll – these are his main variable costs. In contrast, fixed costs are costs that do not vary with the scale of production – for example, the rent of the hot dog stall, which remains the same whether he sells 10 hot dogs or 50.

Let's take a simple example. Say we make hamster wheels that cost €50 each to produce (these are high-quality wheels, obviously), with fixed costs of €50. The total cost – the sum of variable and fixed costs – will rise as more wheels are made. For our limited run of 4 hamster wheels, the total cost rises from €50 when we produce nothing to €250 when we produce 4. If we set the selling price at €200 per wheel, total revenue (price times quantity sold, Q(P)) goes from €0 to €800. The total profit is initially negative, and then rises to €550.

Units sold and produced	0	1	2	3	4
Revenue (@ €200 each)	€0	€200	€400	€600	€800
Fixed costs	€50	€50	€50	€50	€50
Variable costs (@ €50 each)	€0	€50	€100	€150	€200
Total costs	€50	€100	€150	€200	€250
Profit	-€50	€100	€250	€400	€550

However, in reality, fixed costs generally remain fixed only over a specific volume range. Going back to the hot dog example, there is probably a physical limit on how many hot dogs can be produced from a single stall in a working day. Let's say that limit is 100 hot dogs. Therefore, to sell 200 hot dogs, the seller needs to rent a second stall – which increases his fixed costs – but in a 'step' manner – they remain fixed at the rent for a single stall when output is under 100 hot dogs, jump to double the rent for 101 to 200, and jump again to triple for 201 to 300, and so on. So, although fixed costs do increase, economists assume that they are constant over the volume range being considered, in contrast to variable costs, which increase with each and every extra unit of output.

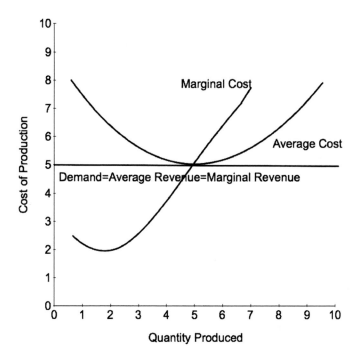

Over the longer run, average fixed and average variable costs of a productive system are generally U-shaped over production ranges. The marginal cost of producing an extra unit of the product generally slopes downwards initially, then shoots upwards as the production system passes the minimum average cost of production, as we see below.

See also

Q6   What are the factors of production?
Q7   What is 'rent'?
Q8   What is marginal analysis?
Q20   What is the 'market'?

Q6　What are the factors of production?

In economics, factors of production – productive inputs – are the resources employed to produce goods and services. They facilitate production but do not become part of the product (unlike raw materials) nor do they become significantly transformed by the production process (unlike fuel used to power machinery).

The main factors of production are:

- Natural resources.
- Labour.
- Capital.

These are combined within effective productive processes by businesses to produce various outputs. The business is assumed to select that combination of inputs from the factors of production that lowers to a minimum its costs of producing its outputs.

Productive resources, in practice, are unlimited in their variety, because no two people or fields or buildings are perfectly alike. The classes into which resources fall are fairly broad, and used only to say something useful about their combination within productive processes. The substitution of capital for labour, when machines replace people, or *vice versa*, defines the patterns of consumption and production within the economy, including the income distribution, and the patterns of combination of the factors of production we can call technology.

See also
Q2　What is an economic model?
Q7　What is 'rent'?
Q41　How does a business decide how much to produce?

Q7   What is 'rent'?

The economic notion of 'rent' goes back to the classical economists of the 18th century, Adam Smith and David Ricardo, who described as rent the amount a capital owner receives from their investments above and beyond what a market in perfect competition would give them. Effectively, it is a measure of the amount capitalists extract from the system by virtue of their position in it. Rent, therefore, is a measure of the difference between a factor's cost to the capitalist and its opportunity cost.

However, 'rent' can be extracted by labour, too. Imagine you are a nuclear scientist. You have trained for 10 years to become knowledgeable in your area. You command a wage above the average, because of your specific skill-set. This extra wage is also 'rent', because you could work instead for minimum wage, or at least for a much lower salary. The professions (medicine, the law, and so forth) ensure their members can extract rent from employers by keeping the cost of entry to the professions high (with exams and limited licensing), and so reducing the supply of entrants, ensuring that the investment made by the individual in gaining admission to the professions is recouped by large salaries.

Marxist economists define the 'circuit of production' around rent. Say you want to build a bread factory. You save up, and buy the flour and the labour of some workers and lease a building to make bread. You sell that bread on the market, and, after paying your costs for inputs to the bread making process, you have some profit (economic rent) left over. You can choose to save that profit, to spend it on yourself, or to reinvest it in a bigger factory, more workers, more wages for the same workers, and so forth. This creates more output (more bread), and if you sell all of that bread, you'll have higher profits (economic rent) again. The 'circuit' of capital is from your initial savings to the ever-expanding process of rent creation.

This circuit can be broken, and can experience cycles, making the system unstable as a result. Say that, instead of reinvesting your own money in the bread factory, you borrowed from someone else. Say now that you do not sell all that extra bread, and cannot service the debt repayments and increased costs of your new factory. The system might collapse if enough people were to have this happen to them. So instability is at the heart of capitalist processes.

See also

Q5   How do economists think about costs?
Q6   What are the factors of production?
Q9   What is opportunity cost?
Q46   What are the major '-isms' in economics?

Q8   What is marginal analysis?

Marginalism is a trend in economics that began in the 19th century. The idea is to use simple tools of calculus to represent an economic decision problem, and to use those tools to find an exact solution.

Take the decision faced by most businesses of how much to produce. If a business could inspect its costs of production at a very fine level – labour by the second, machinery by the bolt, and so on – it could compute the marginal cost of production, that is, the change in the total cost of production when production increases by just one unit.

Typically, marginal cost curves are U-shaped, meaning that the cost of producing the first unit is rather high; the second, much lower; the third, lower still, and so on, until the lowest marginal cost is reached. Then the marginal cost starts to rise, as adding new workers and new plant becomes less and less efficient.

For example, to hire a professor to teach a new course in a university to a single student is prohibitively expensive, since not alone must the professor's salary be paid but also that of perhaps several support staff, as well as provision of the lecture room, teaching aids, IT network, etc. Adding a second student to the class spreads these costs over both students; adding a third spreads the costs even further; to the point where slipping an extra student into a class of 100 students adds virtually no extra cost – the marginal cost of the 101st student is almost nil. But adding a few more students above this either means a new lecture room to accommodate them all, or extra professors to share the teaching load – either way, the marginal cost starts to rise. Hence the U-shaped marginal cost curve.

While marginal analysis often focuses on marginal cost, it also includes marginal benefit.

Think about college grades. Your degree result is usually an average of the marks you get in each course during your final year. Say you normally get a middling 'B' grade in most of your courses. The effect that any one course result, bad or good, has on your overall grade is pretty low.

Similarly, if you are a solid 'D' student, a stellar performance in one module is not going to lift you high enough for a first class degree. The marginal benefit to you is much lower than you might think.

Let's take another small example. Say your gross (before tax) salary is €50,000, and your income is taxed at 25% for the first €20,000, and at 45% from €20,000 to €50,000. How much tax will you pay this year? You'll pay (0.25*20,000) + (0.45*30,000) = 5,000 + 13,500 = €18,500. Your net pay is 50,000-18,500 = €31,500. Monthly, that works out to €2,625.

Now let's say someone offers you another part time job, for €1,000 extra a month, or €12,000 a year. You pay tax at the higher rate, because this is the top slice f income you'll have earned. The *marginal tax* rate on your last €1000 is 45%. So net, after working extra hours, perhaps unsociable hours, not seeing your family and friends, having less leisure time, etc, you will come out with €12,000 - (0.45*€12,000) = €6,600, or €550 per month. Is that worth it? Perhaps it is, perhaps it isn't. It's up to you.

Lots of government policies are determined by looking at the effects marginal tax (or benefit) rates have on incentives. Set the marginal rate too high (say, at 70%) and no one will work harder, causing a decrease in the levels of extra work, and providing a large incentive to find ways to evade this tax, perhaps using criminal means. The loss to the economy could be very large indeed. Set the marginal rate too low, and the government of the day will lose substantial taxation revenue, which may harm government programmes and income redistribution measures like social welfare payments, free childcare and free medical care, and so on. Marginal analysis can be a very powerful and useful policy tool when used correctly.

See also

Q9   What is opportunity cost?

Opportunity cost is a deep economic concept with a simple definition. The opportunity cost of a decision is the value of the next best choice. In other words, the opportunity cost of making a choice to consume something is what you give up by making that choice to get that something – for example, if you have a choice between buying the latest Harry Potter book or seeing a James Bond movie, buying the book means losing the opportunity to see the movie, since you cannot do both.

Opportunity cost is one way economists measure the economic cost of using scarce resources to produce goods in terms of the alternatives foregone by producing these goods. For example, if you choose to produce a product using some combination of food and drink, in the diagram below, the production possibility frontier (or boundary) shows the quantity of food and drink that can be produced with the level of technology and the resources available. If you want to increase production of food from 6 units to 8, then you will have fewer resources to produce drink, production of which declines from 4.6 to 3.2 units. Alternatively, if you are prepared to reduce the production of food to 3 units, production of drink will increase from 4.6 to 6 units.

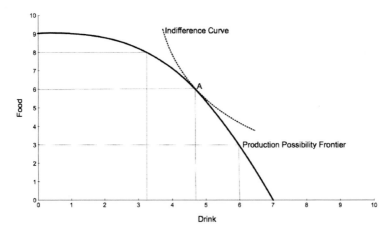

The production possibility frontier

The production possibility frontier shows the marginal rate of transformation between two goods – effectively, the ratio between the marginal costs of producing the two goods. Your preferences between food and drink are represented by the indifference curve – a contour line, along which total utility is constant – which just touches the production possibility frontier at point A and represents your happiness (or utility) from consuming different combinations of food and drink. The further from the origin of the graph an indifference curve is, the higher the total level of utility.

Another example of opportunity cost is time: the opportunity cost of you reading this sentence is the next best thing you could be doing with your time right now. The fact you are choosing to read this line means you think this is the best possible way to spend your time. I'm chuffed!

See also
Q5 How do economists think about costs?
Q8 What is marginal analysis?
Q10 What is utility?

Q10   What is utility?

The concept of utility has a long and convoluted history in economics, and has been discussed since at least 1748. Utility is the satisfaction a person receives from their economic activities.

To get a measure of utility, we need to make some assumptions about the world:

- *Ceteris paribus*: Holding other factors constant, we can think about measuring utility because other choices outside the ones we are considering are not affected by the choices we make now.

- Utility function: There need to be at least two goods in a model of economic choice. Most of the time, there are many more. For each numerical combination of goods (X and Y), the function gives a level of utility (U), holding everything else constant.

We also need to make some assumptions about preferences:

- Transitivity: If there are three goods (X, Y and Z), then the consumer can always choose between them. If he / she prefers X to Y, and prefers Y to Z, then he must prefer X to Z.

- Completeness: For any given list of goods, the consumer must be able to make a choice between those goods, and to rank them, because the assumption of transitivity must hold.

- More preferred to less: If the good is 'normal', when the consumer's income increases, he / she will demand more of it, since consumers always prefer more stuff to less stuff.

These assumptions allow us to draw an indifference curve, which represents a set of points (a locus) where, for each consumer, each point represents a combination of goods that makes them equally happy. Think of an indifference curve like a contour map of a mountain: the consumer will always want to be higher up the mountain of happiness, so to speak, rather than lower down, but once on a contour line, they will be indifferent between the alternative positions on that line.

The slope of the indifference curve shows the marginal rate of substitution – the idea that a consumer will be willing to give up a certain number of units of a good to get more units of another good on the same indifference curve. The marginal rate of substitution is the ratio between the marginal utilities of each good. The marginal rate of substitution stops moving along the indifference curve when the ratio between the prices of each good is equal to the value of the marginal rate of substitution.

The ratio of the extra utility for consuming one more unit of either good to its price should be the same for each good. The budget curve (below) shows the combinations of the two goods the consumer can afford, given that they have a fixed amount of income. The budget curve is downward-sloping because, to get more of good 2, the consumer must give up some of good 1.

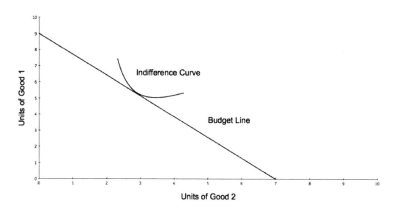

The budget curve.

See also
Q8   What is marginal analysis?
Q9   What is opportunity cost?

Q11 What is a price?

The question of what determines the prices that are paid for goods or services rendered is central to all economic thinking. How are the proceeds from the sale of goods and services distributed? How much of the proceeds of the sale go to wages, and how much to profit, interest, rent of land and other resources? These questions are at the heart of economics.

From the attempt to answer these questions come two different subjects: the theory of value, and the theory of distribution.

Think about prices in very poor societies. These prices reflect the bare essentials of survival, so changing the price of basic foodstuffs like bread and meat can change death rates. In a more affluent society, changing the price of bread or meat leads to a change in behaviour – people simply buy other things, or forego another good to buy the bread.

The context within which the price is expressed matters, too. Prices convey information, which helps you make a decision on whether, given your circumstances – your preferences, your budget, and so on – you want to buy the good or service.

In a market economy, the price of a good is determined by the number of people buying the good and the number of people selling the good. Prices tell businesses what to produce: if people want more of a particular good than the economy is producing, the price of the good rises; if people want less of that good, the price falls.

Imagine a typical street-corner in any city in the world. Say you want to buy water. If there is a shop nearby, filled with bottles of sparkling and still water, the price charged by a person selling water from a stall on the street needs to be very close to the store price, since you and other potential buyers of water have a choice of where to buy it. But, if the store is closed, leaving the street vendor as the only person nearby with water to sell, the price of water is in the street vendor's power. If he can see you are thirsty, what way do you think the price of water will go? And why?

The reason the street vendor fleeced you is because he suddenly acquired monopoly power in his market, for that small period of time. Monopoly is the situation when one seller dominates the market. Our street vendor used that monopoly power by changing the price charged to get more money for himself. To understand monopoly, we have to talk about markets.

It's also important to understand that the most important function of the price of anything is as half of a ratio. The price of something only matters *relative to something else*. I know that the potatoes I'm buying are good value at €2 because down the road they are €3. I know that the car I'm buying is good value because the price comparison website I used tells me so. And so forth. Prices convey information about relative costs, and relative benefits.

Prices also help producers of goods and service discriminate amongst types of consumer. Think about the price of admission to a cinema. For an adult, it is, say, €10. For a child, only €3. Why? The average total cost to the cinema of producing the film to be seen is the same, regardless of whose eyes are clapped on the screen. The simple fact is that kids don't come to cinemas alone. They come in packs, and with a parent or two. So by reducing the price of admission, cinemas actually make more. In internet cafés, during the day the price of usage is lower than at night, because during the day the cafés are frequented by tourists and the unemployed, and during the night, gamers and students use the café. The owners of the café clearly know how to charge to make sure they make the most from their scarce resource.

See also
Q20   What is the 'market'?
Q25   What is market structure?
Q26   Why do monopolies matter?
Q42   How do businesses know how much to increase prices for a product
       or service?

Q12 Why do economists focus on the consumer?

A consumer in economics is a cardinal figure: they are the people who decide. The idea is that consumers know what they want, most of the time, and know how to get it.

There are two stories economists tell about consumers. The first story is that consumers maximise their utility, subject to a budget constraint – in other words, consumers:

- Are good at understanding themselves, in terms of their preferences, and their budgets, at least in the present. So consumers know they prefer apples to bananas, and bananas to coconuts, meaning they will always prefer apples to coconuts.

- Prefer more to less, generally.

- Understand the range of choices available to them at any moment.

- Understand how to rank different choices (5 apples, 2 bananas, 18 coconuts or 8 apples, 8 bananas, 8 coconuts) to obtain the greatest possible utility.

The second story is related to the first, except that where the first story assumes superhuman rationality and computability, an empirically-based view of the consumer sees them held in sway by:

- Their biases (for example, behaving differently when they win than when they lose).

- Past behaviours.

- External forces like advertising.

- Herding effects, like attempting to keep up with the Joneses.

This consumer does not consume what is best for them, because of bounded rationality – they just cannot compute their maximum utility, given the time and information available to them – but also because consumers do not really want to compute anything. Instead, consumers try to reason around the problem by using simple rules (heuristics), which they can employ in specific task environments (like using a shopping list at a supermarket), viewing choices as a problem to be solved, rather than as an outcome to be maximised.

Thus, because consumers know that better goods cost more to produce, they assume that more expensive goods automatically are better – or that branded goods are better than similar unbranded goods.

See also
Q13   Why do economists assume people are rational?
Q14   What is bounded rationality?

Q13   Why do economists assume people are rational?

Economists generally believe that people tend to make decisions in their own best interests. They assume that people have objectives, goals that they want to achieve, and they have a pretty good idea (according to them) of how to achieve them.

A really simple example is brushing your teeth. You know it is good for you to brush your teeth, so you choose a toothbrush, toothpaste, dental floss, and so forth, and a time of the day, to clean your teeth. You have made half a dozen decisions on the way toward fulfilling your objective, and that is fully rational.

Of course, sometimes people have very complicated objectives (to discover the meaning and purpose of life), and very limited information about those objectives. Nonetheless, they persevere.

The notion of simple objectives comes down to needs and desires. Needs are things like food and shelter, without which we would die. The objective to fulfil these needs comes without much thought at all, and most creatures have a 'rational' response to changes in the conditions for getting things like food and shelter, whether they are human or not. Desires are everything else. We don't all want to drive Ferraris – as individuals, we desire different things.

In economic models, the assumption of rationality acts like a knife, cutting through lots of complexity to allow simple mathematical treatments of very complex phenomena. So, for example, the interaction of thousands of households, businesses, workers, banks, central banks, and governments can be modelled using a 'representative' agent that consumes and produces a single good, using just capital and labour. This incredibly unrealistic story only can be told if there is full rationality, in the sense of perfect foresight and knowledge about tastes and desires, on the part of everyone in the society.

See also

Q2 What is an economic model?
Q12 Why do economists focus on the consumer?
Q14 What is bounded rationality?

Q14   What is bounded rationality?

Bounded rationality is a theory of human behaviour that places limits on the computational capacity of individuals. Economists would like to assume a type of 'super rationality', where people have a limitless capacity for calculation of their wants and desires relative to their budget constraints. Bounded rationality relaxes these unrealistic assumptions to focus on how people actually behave, and where they might deviate from this super-rationality.

Have you ever asked yourself why obese smokers exist at all, or why pregnant women, standing outside hospitals, in front of signs showing the effects on newborns of smoking, still smoke? On a lighter note, why do we fall for 'buy one, get one free' offers. Why do we compare our salaries to our co-workers, rather than looking at whether the salary we earn can buy everything we need to live as we would choose?

Although people making choices want to be rational and to make rational decisions, they cannot always do so. Because they cannot deal with the complexity of information they have to process, they take short cuts. Think about a trip to the supermarket. There are tens of thousands of product combinations available for you to buy. Figuring out which combinations would make you happiest (technically, computing the maximum utility of your choice set) each time you went to the supermarket would take hours. Yet it takes minutes to shop. Why? Because you recognise the computational problem, and take a shortcut instead and use a shopping list. People use heuristics, or simple rules of thumb, to make estimates about the frequency of events in the world. Sometimes these estimates can be wildly inaccurate. In the case of the shopping list, you rely on what you bought the last time, which is 'good enough' for you, or on what a friend has recommended, rather than taking the time always to compute the maximum.

Thus, consumers are not always fully rational but operate within bounded rationality. People are prone to excitement, love, grief and jealousy. They follow habits, like smoking and eating too much, which may not be in their best interests long-term. People are irrational investors—they prefer more now relative to later, and expect fairness from others. They also react differently to losses and gains. The current 'hot topic' area in economics is behavioural economics, and bounded rationality underpins all of this.

See also
Q12   Why do economists focus on the consumer?
Q13   Why do economists assume people are rational?

Q15   Why are expectations important?

People's expectations about the future change their behaviour today. If I think I'm going to die in less than five years, will I save by investing in bonds with a 10-year maturity? Of course not. If I am worried that I may be made unemployed, will I increase or decrease my consumption? I'll decrease it, clearly.

Economics has no coherent way to deal with the uncertainty and risk associated with the unknown future. Most economists assume expectations are formed as a result of looking at the past and forecasting out, with some error – these are called extrapolative expectations.

Another idea, called the rational expectations hypothesis, is that, most of the time, people act with the best information about the future they can, and without bias. This hypothesis has been largely discredited in recent years. The important assumption of rational expectations is that investors are risk-neutral, implying that expected returns to different assets in financial markets have to be equal. The lynchpin of this theory is that people can see the future, however imperfectly, and use this 'rational forecast' rather than the simple extrapolation of the past.

Other economists assume adaptive expectations, which complicate matters by constantly changing as time passes.

Overall, economists agree expectations are extremely important in economics, particularly in modelling the business cycle, in financial economics, and in microeconomics. There is, unfortunately, no consensus on how to represent expectations in a formal economic model. Economics is not advanced enough yet to deal with how people actually think about the future.

See also
Q2   What is an economic model?
Q13   Why do economists assume people are rational?
Q38   What is the economic definition of risk – and how does it differ from uncertainty?

Q16   What is consumer surplus?

The consumer surplus is the extra satisfaction a consumer gets by paying the actual price requested by a seller for a product, rather than the maximum amount they would have been prepared to pay.

Imagine you are a die-hard fan of a particular performer, and would pay up to €10 for a ticket to see them perform. Yet, the ticket only costs €5. Your extra satisfaction is the consumer surplus, the lighter shaded area between the offer price and the demand curve in the diagram below:

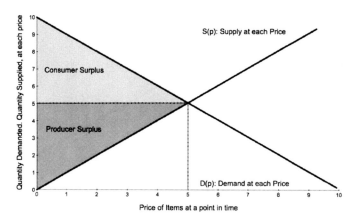

Consumer surplus.

Consumer surplus is greatest only in perfectly competitive markets, where the price of any good is determined by the interplay of supply and demand. Where market price is not determined by perfect competition, say, in a condition of monopoly, where one business sells all of the goods available, then consumer surplus is much, much less.

See also
Q17   What is producer surplus?
Q20   What is the 'market'?

Q17   What is producer surplus?

Producer surplus is the difference between the price the producer gets for their products, and the price they would be willing to sell those products for. Looking at a supply and demand diagram, producer surplus is the darker shaded area between the supply curve and the offer price in the diagram below. The producer surplus is analogous to the consumer surplus: the only difference being who gets the surplus.

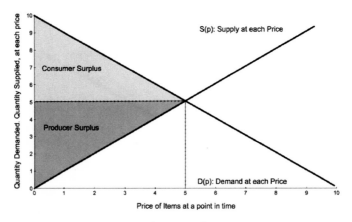

Producer surplus.

Imagine producers decide to increase the price by colluding. The area of the producer surplus will increase, with a corresponding decrease in consumer surplus. There are also 'deadweight' effects to these activities, because increases in price cause a decrease in quantity demanded of any good. This loss is borne by everyone, because the goods are never bought and, in the limit, never produced.

See also
Q16   What is consumer surplus?
Q18   What is a deadweight loss?
Q20   What is the 'market'?

Q18 What is a deadweight loss?

When supply and demand schedules are not in equilibrium, the levels of consumer and producer surplus are not at their highest. A deadweight loss is the net loss of both consumer and producer surplus resulting from an overproduction or underproduction of a product, arising from this lack of equilibrium.

Often, a deadweight loss occurs because of the imposition of a tax on the sale of a good. The diagram below shows the position before the imposition of a tax.

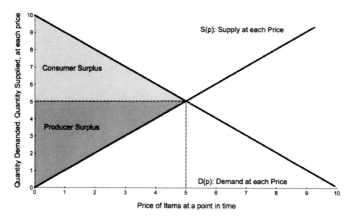

Producer and consumer surplus before the imposition of a tax.

If a tax is imposed, the price the customer sees moves up from €4 to €5, creating a drop in quantity demanded from 6 units to 5, as well as a drop in both consumer and producer surplus.

The area shaded in the second diagram with the label 'dwt' is the deadweight loss of taxation. The government earns taxation revenue, shown in the box titled 'tax' but, because consumer and producer surplus are not at their highest possible levels, the amount lost is a 'deadweight'. No one gains this amount, neither consumers, producers nor the government.

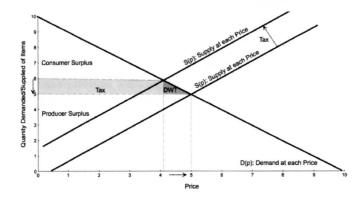

Deadweight loss: The triangle formed by the change in supply schedule, tax revenue, and the original demand schedule.

See also

Q19 What are economic incentives and why do people react to them?

An incentive in economics is anything that directs behaviour in a particular way. The incentive does not have to be a monetary reward, or even something nice that makes the individual or organisation happier – torture is an incentive as well, although it is a coercive incentive. Equally, there are moral incentives not to behave in certain ways – to murder, say, or to torture.

Most of the time, economists are interested in monetary incentives. Monetary incentives exist when individuals believe or expect that acting in a certain way will allow them to increase their personal finances.

For example, in labour markets throughout time, wages of different kinds have been used to direct productive behaviour. From shares of agricultural output in times of serfdom, to barter, to piece rates, to hourly wages regardless of the rate of output, to efficiency wages (where workers are paid above the average to increase output), to profit-shares and other more complex remunerative arrangements, the influence of remuneration on behaviour is the primary study of labour economics.

Incentives can be weak or strong, and may or may not elicit the behaviour expected, because of the law of unintended consequences.

Incentives may also be perverse, where the behaviour seen as a result of the incentive is the opposite of what was intended.

Societal incentives include the need for security, stability, reproduction of society, and the reproduction of norms and customs, which also affect how we behave in our daily lives.

See also
Q13 Why do economists assume people are rational?
Q15 Why are expectations important?

Q20   What is the 'market'?

The 'market' is a metaphor, a way of thinking about practices of exchange between different people in different places, and at different times.

Traditionally, economists thought of market processes as affecting both the supplier of the good – the person behind the stall, selling it – and the demander of the good – the person who purchases that good, at a specific price. Today, the market is seen as just a set of rules governing transactions, whatever those transactions might be. The market has always been seen as unpredictable, volatile, competitive, and powerful and can take many forms.

The essence of any market is its role as a co-ordination mechanism: it connects and reconciles the various competing interests of those who wish to buy at the cheapest price, and those who want to sell at the dearest. The market reduces the complexity of millions of individual decisions – how much to produce, how much to pay workers, how much to deliver, whether to produce at all, whether to buy, whether to sell, and so on. The market's structure is key in determining the price of a good or service.

One of the kernels of economic thinking is that un-regulated markets with no government interference, that let everyone trade up to the point they are happy and do not want to trade anymore, result in a situation where it is impossible to make anyone better off without making someone worse off. This zero-sum model is a theoretical benchmark, but it does allow for a definition of market 'failure', where the market provides less, or more, of a good or service than might be required.

The basic insight of the competitive market is that, with lots of sellers, all doing the same thing, and lots of buyers, all doing the same thing, we end up with more or less the same price. Supply and demand curves converge on the correct price like the blades of a scissors on a piece of paper, as shown below.

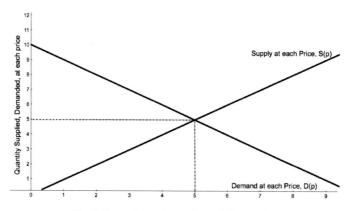

The interaction of supply and demand.

Price is shown on the horizontal (X) axis, and quantity demanded at each price is shown on the vertical (Y). The line sloping downwards from left to right shows how many units buyers would want to buy in the market – this is the demand curve. The line sloping upwards from left to right shows how many units the seller would want to sell – this is the supply curve. (Note that straight lines are considered curves – even though they have no curvature!) In the diagram, at a price of €5, consumers are willing to buy 5 units AND sellers are willing to sell 5 units, as shown by where the demand and supply curves meet – this is the equilibrium point.

If the price increases, then fewer people will be willing to buy the same number of units, and quantity demanded will fall, while quantity supplied will rise, creating a surplus.

If the price falls, then more people will want to buy the units, and fewer people will want to supply them, creating a shortfall.

Imbalances in supply and demand give different incentives to different people in the system, driving prices up and down until a rough equilibrium is reached. The market equilibrium price is reached when the number of items that sellers want to sell is equal to the number of items buyers want to buy.

See also

Q16   What is consumer surplus?

Q17   What is producer surplus?

Q21   What is market failure?

Q22   What is equilibrium?

Q23   What are excess supply and excess demand?

Q42   How do businesses know how much to increase prices for a product
          or service?

Q21   What is market failure?

Market economies are made up of largely self-interested consumers and producers of goods and services. Market failures happen when too much, or too little, of a good or service gets produced, or when a good or service gets misallocated. The best example is street lighting: no one would decide to produce street lighting for a profit, because they cannot limit who uses the lighting by charging those people a price. Thus, the market has failed to supply something people would benefit from.

Market failure often happens in public goods (street lighting), which are different from private goods (chocolate bars) in two main ways:

- Public goods are non-excludable: It is not possible to stop someone who does not pay from consuming the good.
- Public goods are non-subtractible: The same unit of the good can be consumed by more than one person at the same time.

When goods are non-excludable and non-subtractible, the market (through businesses supplying the product or service for profit) will not provide them. The only type of good provided regularly by the market process is private goods. Other types of good require governance, regulation, and perhaps, government intervention, to compensate for the market failure.

The table below, adapted from Ostrom and Ostrom (1977), shows a two-dimensional categorisation of different types of goods.

		Subtractibility	
		Low	High
Exclusion	Hard	Public Goods Useful Knowledge Sunsets	Common Pool Resources Libraries Irrigation systems
	Easy	Toll or Club Goods Journal Subscriptions Daycare centres	Private Goods Personal Computers Doughnuts

Market failures.

These distinctions are very important—much of the legal code, regulation structure, and enforcement, in developed countries is based around trying to turn non-exclusive, non-subtractible goods and services, into exclusive, subtractible goods and services.

Take the problem of enclosing land. Previous to the Enclosure Acts beginning in the 1770s (and onward) in Great Britain, everyone had the right to graze their animals on any available fields. Land was a public good, which was difficult to exclude, and where subtractibility was high. With the stroke of a pen (or perhaps a quill!), land became a private good, with fences clearly delimiting the 'private' from the 'public' spaces. Suddenly land was 'mine', and not 'ours', and with these acts the regime of private property as the foundation for modern economies was born.

See also
Q20   What is the 'market'?
Q22   What is equilibrium?
Q23   What are excess supply and excess demand?

Q22   What is equilibrium?

The word 'equilibrium' is a loaded term in economics. Mathematically, equilibrium is a point of stability, of balance, that does not change over time. An economy – or any other system – is in equilibrium if it would continue in its present state forever without changing, unless some outside force disturbed it. A ball resting at the bottom of a hollow is in equilibrium. The equilibrium price of an item in an unregulated market is the point at which the amount supplied is equal to that demanded. In economics, markets are assumed to generate forces that provide tendencies towards equilibrium over time. If there are some inherent forces that will always cause change, then the economy is not in an equilibrium.

For example, imagine the 'true' price of an item is €4. The seller wants €10 for it. Over time, because no one wants to buy the item at that price, the seller will be forced to lower their price closer and closer to €4, perhaps even passing €4 on the way down, and then increasing the price back to €4.

The basic insight is very simple: prices adjust until the amount that people demand of something is equal to the amount that is supplied.

This basic insight is complicated when market participants have limited information, when they cannot process all supply and demand bids equally, and when a condition called 'bounded rationality' applies.

See also
Q5   How do economists think about costs?
Q20   What is the 'market'?
Q21   What is market failure?
Q23   What are excess supply and excess demand?

Q23   What are excess supply and excess demand?

When markets are in disequilibrium, and demand exceeds supply, there are shortages of wanted goods and services. This is a condition of excess demand.

When supply exceeds demand, there is excess supply, and gluts of too many produced items.

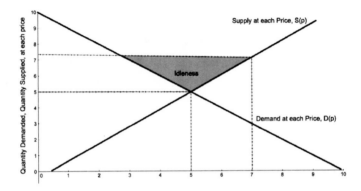

In both cases of excess demand and supply, the price mechanism of the market can help to reduce the shortage by increasing prices and bidding up suppliers' willingness to supply for a profit, while in excess supply, the price can fall sufficiently so that the excess stock is cleared during a series of fire sales. Eventually, the interaction of supply and demand will move the market to a state of equilibrium.

See also
Q20   What is the 'market'?
Q21   What is market failure?
Q22   What is equilibrium?

Q24   What are comparative statics?

Something is static if it does not move. Economics typically looks for simple models that produce equilibrium, a point of balance between competing forces. Once an equilibrium is found, the model is tested by changing some of the variables within the model, or from outside the model, to see what happens.

Comparative statics is the study of how the solutions of an economic model change as a model's parameters and specifications are changed. Comparative statics is very important in economic analysis, because most of the testable predictions of economic theory are comparative statics predictions. Also, many quantitative economic equilibrium analyses are built from comparative statics analyses of a model's components. The results of comparative statics analyses form the basis for much of our understanding of the behaviour of the economy.

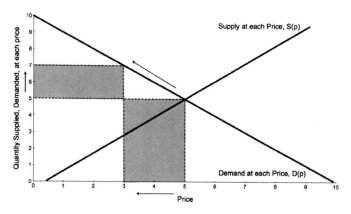

Comparative static analysis.

For example, imagine a change in the price of a good on the supply and demand of that good. When prices rise, people demand less of the good, and suppliers are willing to supply more of it, ending up with a surplus of the good. When prices fall, people demand more of the good, while suppliers want to produce less of it, ending up with a shortage.

Comparative statics compares the situation at different price points to develop the graph above.

See also
Q2   What is an economic model?

Q25 What is market structure?

The structure of any market is defined by the number and size of producers and consumers in the market, the type of goods and services being traded, and the degree to which information can flow freely.

In the real world, we can identify several types of market structure:

- Monopoly: Here there is only one provider of a product or service. For example, electricity provision in most countries.

- Natural monopoly: A monopoly in which economies of scale cause productive efficiency to increase continuously with the size of the business. For example, the canal system in 19th century Great Britain.

- Monopolistic competition: Here there are a small number of dependent businesses that, between them, have a very large proportion of the market share. The products from these companies are distinguishable from each other, and these companies attempt to compete with one another. A good example is the restaurant industry in New York City.

- Oligopoly: Here the market is dominated by a small number of businesses that own more than 40% of the market share. A good example is the Mobile Phone industry in the United States, and in Europe.

- Duopoly: This is a special case of oligopoly, where there are only two businesses in the marketplace and, as a result, each business has a very large level of market power. The competition between Visa and MasterCard in the credit card industry is a good example of duopoly.

- Oligopsony: This is the opposite of oligopoly – although there are now many sellers, there are only a few buyers. Here the fast food industry, with a few major buyers like McDonalds and Burger King, has a lot of power over the many sellers of meat, chicken, and potatoes that make up their sandwiches.

- Monopsony: This occurs when there is only one buyer in the market. The best example is professional baseball. If you are very talented at baseball, then there is only one market to sell your services---the United States. Many athletic industries share similar traits to Major League Baseball.

The theoretical ideal is a perfectly competitive market in which there are many buyer and many sellers, none of whom exercise any special power in the marketplace, and all of whom have perfect information about what's happening in the marketplace.

See also
Q20   What is the 'market'?
Q26   Why do monopolies matter?

Q26 Why do monopolies matter?

A monopoly is a market structure where only one business (or person) supplies that market. In that sense, monopolies are best described by what they don't have: competition. The monopolist has market power— they can charge what price they like relative to their costs, and make the largest profits possible for themselves.

Monopoly is contrasted with perfect competition, where no one has any market power. In a perfectly competitive market, there are no barriers to entry, no informational problems, or product differentiation.

Monopolists earn economic 'rent', or profits well in excess of any normal profits, and they can use these rents in different ways. Sometimes, the rent is spent on research and development, and may result in innovation and new products and services. Sometimes, the rent is spent on keeping barriers to entry high – for example, by lobbying government to stop any new entrants to the market the monopolist currently dominates.

Monopolies matter because they can harm society if their goals and objectives move in a different way to society's.

The monopolist charges consumers far more for the same product than a set of perfectly competitive businesses might, and generally restricts output of its products. Society could gain from increased output of the product. The social cost of additional inputs shunted into this one industry would be less than the social benefit we might get from any additional output.

Or take a polluting monopolist, whose output is poisoning the environment of the society in which it exercises its market power. It may be difficult to regulate the monopolist in this situation.

See also
Q7 What is 'rent'?
Q25 What is market structure?

Q27   What is aggregate demand / supply?

Every market, if it operates for long enough, generates demand and supply curves.

The aggregate demand for all goods and services in the economy in a given year is the total amount of expenditure by the different sectors of society. Thus, aggregate demand is the sum of all consumption expenditure, investment, government expenditure, and net exports (exports – imports) in the economy. Changes in aggregate demand can lead to changes in the growth rate of the economy, which can generate business cycles. The aggregate demand schedule interacts with the aggregate supply schedule to determine overall national income and output.

The aggregate supply schedule shows the total amount of goods and services supplied to the economy by businesses, households, and the government, in a given year.

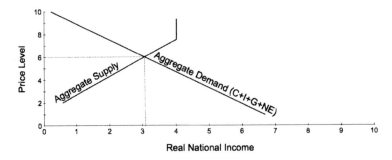

The interaction of aggregate demand and aggregate supply.

The interaction of aggregate demand and supply is shown in the diagram above. The overall price level in the economy is shown on the vertical axis. The level of economic output of goods and services is shown on the horizontal axis. There is a limit to the amount any economy can supply, so the aggregate supply schedule slopes vertically upwards at the end, since the economy cannot produce beyond this point.

For a given price level, aggregate demand and aggregate supply interact to produce a particular level of national income. If the price level changes (if there is inflation in the economy due to a war, or at a point in the business cycle like an economic boom, say), then aggregate demand will shift backwards towards the horizontal axis, because consumption (C) and Investment (I) will be depressed by higher prices. Economic income will fall as a result.

See also
Q72 What is the business cycle?
Q73 How fast should an economy grow?

Q28 Why are the supply chains of some companies more connected than others?

Vertical integration is a type of business structure where one business controls large parts of the supply chain of the product it produces and sells. For example, some oil companies explore and drill for oil, extract it from the ground or sea-bed, refine it to make a range of products (petrol, heating oil, etc), and sell these products directly into the marketplace under their own brand.

Vertical integration is a way to reduce transportation and distribution costs, as well as to derive economies of scale. Businesses can increase supply chain quality by enforcing common standards, and can create 'ripple down' efficiencies, where an innovation in one area of the business gets transferred to the rest of the supply chain. So, although the business might contract out some of its functions to other businesses, most of the components are specified, produced, and shipped in-house.

However, vertical integration carries risks for businesses. Vertically-integrated businesses are more exposed to changes in demand: because the demand is for a final product, when a drop in demand comes, the ripple effect back through the various divisions of the business is very strongly felt.

See also
Q40 How does the behavioural theory of the business explain how businesses work?

Q29 What is a barrier to entry or exit?

A barrier to entry is an advantage of established sellers in an industry over potential entrant sellers, which is reflected in the extent to which established sellers persistently can raise their prices above competitive levels without attracting new businesses to enter the industry.

One barrier to entry is that incumbent businesses have the advantage of lower cost, because they know what they are doing through years of experience and can do it more efficiently than a new entrant. They may also have sufficient sales to give them economies of scale unavailable to a new entrant.

Another barrier is that consumer preferences initially will be with the incumbent(s) due to branding, and product lock-ins. A further barrier to entry might be large capital expenditures, or harsh licensing requirements within a sector. Another barrier to entry might be the incumbent businesses themselves, although anti-trust laws attempt to prevent uncompetitive practices.

A barrier to exit may exist when a legal or economic imperative forces a company to stay in one market. Examples include a high fixed cost to leaving – say, the demolition of a large plant, or large redundancy costs, or environmental clean-up costs, or the expectation that one day the market may recover. Finally, there is national pride.

An example of barriers to exit is the Japanese rice industry. Most of Japan's rice comes from elsewhere—the Japanese consume far more rice than is grown in their country. The land value in Japan is very high, so the opportunity cost of producing the rice is very high. National pride, however, stops the uncompetitive rice industry from failing, and so it is propped up by protectionist subsidies from the Japanese government.

Another example of barriers to exit is the steel production in the United States. The plant required for steel production is very specific, and would not be transferable. The redundancy costs of losing steel production would be very high – socially, economically, and politically – and so, the United States keeps its steel industry alive with subsidies.

See also
Q25 What is market structure?

Q30   What is game theory and how does it help to make people better off?

Game theory is the study of strategic interaction. Developed in the 1950s, game theory developed a series of concepts around the notion of the 'game', where a set of players face incentives similar to those faced by real world actors. The players try to do the best they can in any given situation, given what they think everyone else is doing. Each individual has to consider how their own behaviour affects the attainment of a point of balance, or equilibrium.

There are games of complete information, where everyone knows everything, including the benefits to different courses of action taken by other players, and games of incomplete information, when individual players do not know as much about their rivals, and cannot put themselves in other players' shoes as easily. There are also evolutionary games, where players learn behaviour, and infinitely long games, where players know and expect they will play forever.

Each game has a set of players, who have various strategies allotted to them under the rules of the game. Each set of strategies is associated with a set of payoffs. The payoffs to each player are normally represented as a matrix, as below. For example, in a two-player game, imagine the game revolves around driving either on the left-hand side of the road or the right. Neither player cares which side they drive on – they just do not want to crash into one another. Player 1's payoffs come first, so in the top left-hand entry, (10, 10) is a positive payment of 10 to player 1, and then a payment of 10 to player 2, who have both chosen to 'play' by driving on the left-hand side of the road.

		Player 2	
		Left	Right
Player 1	Left	10,10	-10, -10
	Right	-10, -10	10, 10

A game's payoff matrix.

If both players pick the same side to drive on (either left or right, as long as both choose it), they do well, getting where they want to go, and so earning +10 each. But, if they differ in their decision, then things may go badly for them, and they may crash, costing them -10 each. The matrix shows these payoffs.

The strategies involved here are fairly simple for each player:

- Always play left.
- Always play right.
- Play left if the other player plays left
- Play right if the other player plays right.

In fact, in games like this, where each player must choose at the same time, the number of 'pure' strategies available to each player must be equal to the number of scenarios available. The equilibrium in this game is called a 'Nash equilibrium', after mathematician John Nash. The Nash equilibrium is the best response of each player to each other player's best moves. There can be multiple equilibria, as there are in this game: the best response for player 1 to player 2 playing Left is to play Left, and similarly for player 1 playing Right.

See also
Q32   What is arbitrage?

Q31   What is an index?

An index is a measurement device, used to compare variables with one another, relative to some common reference.

The best use of an economic index is in growth: we wish to measure the performance of the economy today, relative to yesterday, in terms of the quantity of output produced (by GDP). But prices might have changed since the first measurement date. We need a way of expressing the change in output in terms of a common price system. The easiest way to do this is to take the prices from yesterday, multiply them by the quantities today, and thus make the quantity of output produced today easily comparable to yesterday's.

For example, say there are two goods being produced: masks and chain saws. The prices and quantities of each good across two periods are shown below.

Year	Chain Saws			Masks			GDP (€)
	Price (€)	Quantity	Total (€)	Price (€)	Quantity	Total (€)	
2010	10	15	150	3	50	150	300
2011	8	20	160	4	45	180	340

Index numbers.

In 2010, chain saws count for 10 units of GDP, but for only 8 in 2011. Masks count for 3 units of GDP in 2010, and for 4 in 2011. We need units common to both years. We could choose either 2010 or 2011 prices as units of measurement.

If we choose 2010 as the base year, we would re-value units produced in 2011 at 2010 prices. So, instead of the 2011 prices of €8 per chainsaw and €4 per mask, we multiply the product as follows:

€10 * 20 +€3 * 45 = €335 in relative prices.

We can see that the measure of output is reduced correspondingly.

Indices are very common in economics. Indices are used to measure and compare the economic outputs of different countries, of income inequality within and between countries, of environmental degradation in regions, to compare price changes over time and between countries, and many more.

See also
Q50   What is inflation?
Q70   What is Gross Domestic Product?

Q32   What is arbitrage?

Arbitrage occurs when assets are sold in different markets for different prices and a buyer buys an asset in one market and sells it in another to obtain riskless profits.

Take the market for cars, for example. You can go to your local dealer, and pay €20,000 for a specific model. However, if another dealer was selling the same model for a lower price (say, €19,000), you could buy the cheaper car, and sell it to the first dealer, making a sure and easy profit of €1,000 (this assumes, of course, that your local dealer does not intend to make a profit himself on the further sale of the car).

Of course, once you have bought the car, the arbitrage opportunity ceases to exist – because, as soon as the second dealer works out what you are doing, he will put up the price of the car to €20,000. True arbitrage opportunities are few and far between, because once identified, they disappear with alarming speed.

Arbitrage is assumed to occur in every market, but in particular it is present in financial markets, where there are lots of potential buyers and sellers with lots of information about the quality of the assets they are purchasing. The arbitrage process is really a set of transactions such that it requires non-positive initial investment and gives the participants in the process non-negative payoffs. Someone must do well out of the process for it to be an arbitrage.

See also

Q33   What is economic geography?

Economic geography is the study of spatial effects on economic decisions. The idea of economic geography is to analyse the effects of space, place, and scale when economic actors make their decisions. Some places are better for digging diamond mines than others, and are hence more valuable. Some places have flows of goods and services between other places that make them very valuable. Some scales are more important that others – national, regional, city, and local scales all have different constraints, and all have a bearing on the investment decision.

Most of modern economics has nothing to say about geography. Economics is concerned with the consumption, production and distribution of the goods and services of a society over time. Economics is a social science built around the notion that rational actors will do the best they can for themselves most of the time, and they will maximise the benefits to society as a whole while doing so. The classical economists – Smith, Ricardo, Marx, and Malthus – were concerned with how labour and investible capital might be combined in space, and why factories, towns, and households located where they did. However, following the mathematisation of economics by Lèon Walras and Alfred Marshall, space became just another factor of production, like labour, and the importance of location was subsumed within elegant mathematical models of rational behaviour.

So economics discovered, and then forgot, geography. For a time.

Interest in why businesses locate where they do, and why, was rekindled by the statistician Harold Hotelling in 1929. Hotelling imagined two businesses at opposite ends of a straight road, with houses located between the two businesses. The people in each house had to choose whether to travel to the first business, or to the second. Depending on the distance from their house, the person incurred a cost in travelling. The business located closest to the most houses, or the business with the lowest unit prices for its good, won, and drove the other out of business. Hotelling's model was a special case of the Median Voter Theorem, and has been used in many aspects of social science.

In the 1950s, economic geography allied itself with development economics – why some countries are rich, and others are poor, and what to do about it – and became a niche subject. All that changed when Paul Krugman, already famous for his work in international trade, reinvigorated economic geography in 1991 with a paper that would win him the Nobel Prize in economics in 2008. The 'New Economic Geography' now sits at the centre of most economic models of production, and is now a mature field within economics. At the cutting edge, economics has rediscovered geography, yet again, and it is trickling slowly down to the textbooks. But beware: nothing is ever learned for long.

There is also much controversy between economists who study economic geography, and geographers who study the economy. Economists tend to model the location and production decisions of businesses and households, and little more. Geographers take a multi-faceted view of the problem, looking at the wider context in which economic transactions take place.

Despite the controversy, economic geography is very useful in understanding *why* businesses choose to locate their plant and machinery in one country and not another. It explains why we see clustering effects within regions and by industry, and it is a good guide for the development of policies and industrial development strategies.

See also
Q74 What is economic development?

Q34   What is an economic identity?

An economic identity is a way to show an enduring relationship between two variables, which are equal by definition.

Identities pop up a lot in economics. The simplest are of the form: €1 = 100 cents, but some can be controversial. There is a theory called the quantity theory of money, which says that money supply M, times the velocity of circulation, V, is directly related to the price level P times the output of the economy, Y, all of which is expressed as:

$$M.V \cong P.Y$$

This identity is controversial in economics, because the logical next step, if you believe this is a true representation of the world, is to try to control the economy's level of output by controlling the supply of money in the economy. It implies a restricted role for fiscal policy and government intervention in stabilising the economy. The set of policies this identity leads to is called 'monetarism'.

So, an identity in economics is extremely important, because from these basic assumptions or postulates comes an enormously beneficial or costly policy prescription, which can help or damage the lives of millions.

See also
Q35   Why do economists use graphs?
Q36   Why do economists use equations and functions to explain their theories?
Q77   Why does fiscal policy matter?

Q35   Why do economists use graphs?

A graph is one way to represent data and their relationship to one another. Graphs and diagrams are very important in economics. They are used to display economic data, to display the important economic forces at work (say in a supply and demand diagram), to work out the effects of changing these forces (say an increase in price), and to work out, without any mathematics, what the end result might be. Graphs in economics are used as representations of reality, and representations of economists' ideas about reality. Sometimes a graph will be used to illustrate a two-dimensional example of a larger economic problem, and sometimes as a corollary for much more abstract economic theorems.

Most importantly, figures and graphs are expository devices in economics. They are used to explain, to persuade, to teach, and to convince. As an example, here is the supply and demand diagram, the most famous graph in economics.

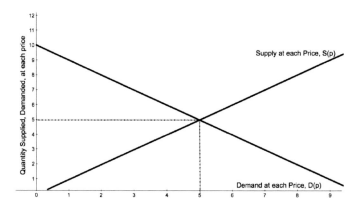

Here's how to read a graph of a variable changing over time – use the example figure below as a guide. First, look at the title of the thing: what does it think it is describing? Look for subjects, and for dates. For example, one would like to see Real Gross Domestic Product, 1967-2010, United States as a title. The line you'll be looking at, if it is a line graph, will tell you about the movement of inflation-adjusted GDP over a defined time range. The next thing to work out are the axes – what is being measured? It is billions of US dollars? Is it a change over time? It is on a logarithmic scale? Then look at the lines within the graph. Do they change abruptly? Does the line tend upwards or downwards over time?

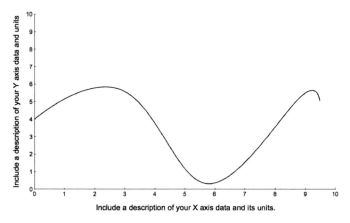

Include a description of your X axis data and its units.

The line in the graph represents an economic relationship.

Finally, because economics uses graphs endlessly; it is worth getting to know how they work, and how to construct one. When making a graph, first check the data. Remember the maxim: garbage in, garbage out. If your data are correct, then make sure to explain your encodings, label both the vertical and horizontal axes, and ensure you use and explain units, and make sure to keep your geometry in check. Show the source of your data, so those readers who are interested can check your findings, and expand on them if they like.

See also
Q34   What is an economic identity?
Q36   Why do economists use equations and functions to explain their theories?
Q37   What are good sources of economic data?

Q36 Why do economists use equations and functions to explain their theories?

Economists love equations. They make us feel like real scientists. Sadly, most of economic life is not well described by equations, but we persevere.

Equations are mathematical sentences, which say that the expression on the right-hand side of the equals sign is equal to the expression on the left-hand side. Models are causal stories economists generate to fit the patterns they see in the data; an equation is part of the modelling toolbox.

A function is a mathematical machine, a process that takes an input and produces an output. For every value of the independent variable, x, within the domain of the function, there is one value for the dependent variable, y.

Take the function $y = x + 2$. For every number you pump in to the variable x (for example: $x = 1, 2, 3, 4, 5$), the function gives you a corresponding number for y ($y = 3, 4, 5, 6, 7$).

Why are functions useful? Economics is about relationships: between households and businesses, individuals and societies, government and markets, the past and the future, savings and investment, and many more. Functions help us to see these relationships, one variable to another (or many more), so we can talk of a consumption function, which tells us what level of consumption a household will be likely to do in a particular period, given its current level of disposable income.

Functions are used to try to estimate these relationships using real-world data and, most of the time, these functions are represented on graphs to illustrate the relationships.

See also
Q2 What is an economic model?
Q34 What is an economic identity?

Q35   Why do economists use graphs?
Q37   What are good sources of economic data?

Q37 What are good sources of economic data?

Data in economics come from three different sources:

- Governments and other bodies.
- Database businesses.
- Experiments by researchers.

Governments and international bodies collect lots of data. So, the Bureau of Labor Statistics (www.bls.gov) in the US is a good resource for US macroeconomic and microeconomic data. The OECD (www.oecd.org) is an excellent source of national data across the developed world. Eurostat provides data on the Eurozone at ec.europa.eu/Eurostat. A new World Bank service (data.worldbank.org) promises to provide a huge resource for economists. Google provides lots of data on the financial markets *via* finance.google.com, and on macro-economics *via* data.google.com. Generally, when looking for macro-type data, look first at the international bodies, then at the nations themselves you happen to be interested in. Much of this information is freely available.

The next type of data is available from financial publishers or database businesses, which collect specialised information with a view to reselling it. This data is harder to access for free, and also may require lots of data-mining before it can be of use. The important part of any empirical exercise with this kind of data is to compare and contrast it with either previous eras or with other entities experiencing the same conditions. Say, for example, you want to study price changes in copper mining. The Reuters and Bloomberg services will carry the price data but, to give it context, some reading is required to establish the context for the study, and comparative statistical research – on other commodities, say, or other industries within the same country – will prove invaluable.

The final type of economic data you will encounter is bespoke experimental data, which at the moment is much harder to find, but which will become more prevalent in the coming years.

See also

Q35 Why do economists use graphs?

Q36 Why do economists use equations and functions to explain their theories?

Q38 What is the economic definition of risk – and how does it differ from uncertainty?

Economists distinguish between risk and uncertainty. The risk of an event occurring is linked to the probability of it occurring. If risk increases, then the likelihood of an adverse outcome or loss increases.

Some risks are quantifiable, like the chances of being diagnosed with cancer or having your house robbed. Because these risks are quantifiable, we can insure ourselves against them happening. Other risks are not quantifiable, such as the risk of having a meteor crash into your house, killing you and your family, or the risk of a very sudden movement on the stock exchange wiping out all your wealth. These are such low-probability events that no insurance or hedge can cover their eventuality.

An example: let's say you know you will invest some money. If the outcome of your investment is uncertain, but you've an idea of how likely it is that different outcomes will occur, then your investment is characterised by a quantifiable level of risk. If there was a 50% chance that your income will be €4,500 this year, and a 50% chance your income will be €5,500 this year, then the 'risk' is easy to judge. Risk is not the same thing as uncertainty.

True uncertainty occurs when one cannot even judge how low the probability of an event occurring might be. These are situations in which no repetitive behaviour is present to guide our actions, and no insurance for loss is possible. Examples of fundamental uncertainty might be global warming, the 9/11 attacks, or the launch of a completely new product that creates a new market. So you don't know how likely various events are, and you don't even know what the events are, or the outcomes from those events. In situations of true uncertainty, we simply do not know.

See also
Q15 Why are expectations important?
Q39 What is risk aversion?

Q39　What is risk aversion?

Flip a coin. If the coin isn't tampered with in any way, there are two equally likely outcomes: heads or tails. Placing a bet on each outcome should be easy, because this game is fair: there is an equal likelihood of failure as well as success.

However, a risk-averse person would *not* take this bet, preferring instead to choose only bets that are less risky (and thus more certain) than a fair bet. Risk-neutral people would be indifferent between taking a fair bet and not, and risk-loving people would require no risk premium. They would just take the bet, even if it was not fair to them.

Another way to think about risk aversion is that risk-averse investors are only prepared to take on increased risk if there is a good prospect of increasing their return to compensate them for the increased risk. This person would prefer more of an expected return on their investment to less, of course, and prefer less risk to more, all things being equal.

See also
Q14　What is bounded rationality?
Q38　What is the economic definition of risk – and how does it differ from uncertainty?

MICRO-
ECONOMICS

Q40   How does the behavioural theory of the business explain how businesses work?

Many descriptions of the business focus on its need to extract the greatest profit (the difference between its revenue and its costs). Other descriptions of business behaviour focus on decisions made under uncertainty, where people possess limited cognitive ability and so can exercise only bounded rationality when making decisions. Individuals and groups working in businesses will tend to 'satisfice' – to attempt to attain realistic goals, instead of trying to extract maximum profit.

In the real world, businesses do not just try to maximise their profits. Every business exists in a sea of uncertainty - they simply do not know what will come next. Their information about their world is limited and, even if that information were unlimited, their ability to process all of the relevant information is extremely limited. The business does not exist to clear market prices, but in fact exists merely to continue existing. Unlike the story presented above, businesses are not interested in market clearing prices, nor will their actions, at least in most markets, lead to an equilibrating solution in other markets.

The first goal of any business is to survive until the next year. The second goal is to accumulate power. Power over its customers, its suppliers, its rivals, potential new entrants, the government, the legal and regulatory environment, the natural environment, even the future. The business seeks this power in order to continue to improve its odds of survival into the future. The best way to ensure survival is to grow. The business is therefore incentivised to grow as fast as it can: to be a growth-maximiser.

The benefits of business size growth are pretty obvious: higher salaries, job security, prestige, company planes and cars, and high social status. Importantly, the larger a business is relative to other businesses in its sector (or market), the larger its influence on prices and costs, as well as commuters and communities.

Under conditions of uncertainty, with imperfect market structure, it makes sense to think of the business as searching for a set of cost curves which (it thinks) will guarantee its survival into tomorrow. The fact is that, in any period, any one business can only borrow a finite amount of money, and this amount is usually based on the amount of internal funds the business has accumulated in previous periods. So, retained earnings become important to model for a realistic description of the business. The principle of increasing risk holds that the higher the gearing or leverage ratio (externally generated funds/internally generated funds), the larger the potential volatility of earnings net of interest payments. Businesses, in normal times, are free to borrow what they like at the current rate as a multiple of their previous retained earnings. In crisis periods, this reverses, and the multiple becomes a divisor, perhaps driving businesses out of business (no pun intended).

See also

Q5   How do economists think about costs?
Q14   What is bounded rationality?
Q22   What is equilibrium?
Q38   What is the economic definition of risk – and how does it differ from uncertainty?
Q41   How does a business decide how much to produce?
Q42   How do businesses know how much to increase prices for a product or service?
Q53   How do businesses decide which projects to fund, and which ones to drop?

Q41   How does a business decide how much to produce?

Despite many, many variations across time, across countries, and even across regions, every one producing anything commercially must follow the logic of this simple, stark, equation:

INPUT   ➔   OUTPUT

Raw Materials + Labour + Machinery   ➔   Product + Profit

Every business needs to get its raw materials, labour, and machinery at the lowest price it can, and use the best available technology to combine these elements somehow into a product it can sell to the markets at a price high enough to compensate its employees with wages, and pay the rent on its plant and machinery, as well as other overhead costs.

From the point of view of the economy as a whole, there is no difference between workers and machinery. Labour sometimes is thought of as a substitute for capital, the economist's shorthand for machinery and raw materials. This means that, if a better production technology is available, which produces the product at a lower cost but uses more machinery and fewer workers, then the employer will let workers go as the new machines are bought and come online. And when production lines become expensive to run, they can be switched off, and the workers laid off.

However, the cost to the organisation is different to the cost to society. Workers who become unemployed represent a direct cost to the State through increased claims of unemployment benefit but also, indirectly, through the negative effects unemployment can have on individuals and their families. Notice the difference: production lines, when switched off, do not have these extra costs. Labour does. Labour is special as a result. Which is why unions, employment legislation, and training agencies exist: to help ease and facilitate the transition from one job to another. This distinction is important, because it can sometimes be tempting to think of labour as a good substitute for capital.

There are several stories describing how much a business decides to produce. Most run like this: Businesses know their cost base, and, in the presence of lots of competition, they vary the proportion of capital and labour until they get the lowest cost combination possible with a given level of technology. This is called marginal analysis.

Other stories focus on the business attempting first, just to survive, and second, when the business is making some money, to expand itself. The benefits of business size growth include higher salaries, job security, prestige, company planes and cars, and high social status. Importantly, the larger a business is relative to other businesses in its sector (or market), the larger its influence on prices and costs, as well as on communities.

See also

Q6   What are the factors of production?
Q8   What is marginal analysis?
Q40   How does the behavioural theory of the business explain how businesses work?
Q42   How do businesses know how much to increase prices for a product or service?
Q53   How do businesses decide which projects to fund, and which ones to drop?

Q42   How do businesses know how much to increase prices for a product or service?

The elasticity measure is very important in economics. Elasticities measure the responsiveness of price or income to changes in demand, supply, availability of acceptable substitutes, and time.

Mathematically, the elasticity of demand with respect to a change in price is the percentage change in the quantity of the product demanded for each 1% change in its price. Representing Q_1 as the first measured quantity and Q_2 as the second measured quantity, and P_1 as the first measured price, and P_2 as the second, the formula for the elasticity is given by:

$$E_d = \frac{\dfrac{Q_2 - Q_1}{(Q_2 + Q_1)/2}}{\dfrac{P_2 - P_1}{(P_2 + P_1)/2}}$$

To see how useful the elasticity concept is, imagine you run a summer school, and charge €30 a week for entry. You get more than 100 children in the first week applying, but you take only 100. Encouraged by your success, next week, you decide to increase the price to €50 per week. This time, you get only 80 applying. Calculating the price elasticity of demand for the summer school, you see that

(80-100)/90/(50-30)/40 = -0.44.

You're still taking in more money (€300 versus €400), and you have fewer kids to mind. Overall, a win for you.

If you're wondering where the 90 and 40 came in the formula, it's because I used the arc elasticity representation. It is usually better to calculate the arc elasticity, because this is symmetric with respect to the two prices and two quantities, independent of the units of measurement, and yields a value of unity if the total revenues at two points are equal.

To see this, try for yourself to figure out how high prices should go to make the total revenues equal to one another.

The table below shows some of the features of the price elasticity of demand (PED).

Feature	Elastic goods	Inelastic goods
PED value	Greater than 1	Less than 1
A rise in price means	A larger fall in demand	A smaller fall in demand
Slope of demand curve	Flat	Steep
Number of substitutes	Many	Few
Type of good	Luxury	Necessity
Price of good	Expensive	Cheap
Example	Lexus cars	Petrol

Features of Price Elasticity of Demand.

See also
Q40 How does the behavioural theory of the business explain how businesses work?
Q43 What happens to demand for gin when the price of tonic changes?
Q53 How do businesses decide which projects to fund, and which ones to drop?

Q43   What happens to demand for gin when the price of tonic changes?

Elastic and inelastic goods often interact with one another. The cross-elasticity of demand measures the responsiveness of demand for one good (gin) to a given change in the price of a second good (tonic). We calculate the cross-elasticity as:

Cross-elasticity   =   Percentage change in quantity demanded of gin / Percentage change in the price of tonic.

If the cross-elasticity is positive, then the two goods are substitutes. If is negative, then the two goods are complements.

Two goods are substitutes if, when the price of one rises, demand for the other increases. Examples of substitutes are Mercedes and BMW cars, both luxury brands. If the price of a specific Mercedes model rises, buyers will switch to the now cheaper, equivalent BMW model.

Two goods are complements if, when the price of one rises, demand for the other decreases. Examples of complements are fish and chips. If the price of fish rises, the quantity demanded falls, and the quantity of chips demanded also falls — as few people want to eat just chips without fish.

Using the simple cross-elasticity equation of: Cross-elasticity = Percentage change in quantity demanded of gin / Percentage change in the price of tonic, do you think the cross elasticity will be negative, or positive?

See also
Q41   How does a business decide how much to produce?
Q42   How do businesses know how much to increase prices for a product or service?

Q44   What is break-even analysis?

Businesses try to make profits – you do not need a book on economics to tell you that. How do businesses figure out when they've made a profit? When revenue is equal to costs, at the break-even point where no profit is made, but no losses are being made either. Any amount produced above the break-even line results in a profit.

To determine the *number of units of the product* you need to sell to break-even, calculate the average annual fixed cost/(average per unit sales price less average per unit variable cost).

To determine the *sales value* you have to achieve to break-even, work out the annual fixed cost/(1 - (average per unit variable cost ÷ average per unit sales price)).

For example, imagine a new brewery selling one type of beer, with an average sale price of €20 per keg. The average variable cost for the keg is €8, and the annual fixed costs are €100,000. To break-even, 6,250 kegs – 100,000 / (20-8) = 6,250 kegs – need to be sold. The break-even sales value is €166,666 – calculated as 100,000 / (1 - (8 / 20) = €166,666. No profits will be made by this brewery until 6,250 kegs have been sold, with more than €166,666 in gross sales realised.

Break-even analysis is used extensively in business, and also in the public sector, where the impacts of running new programmes and policies are costed to estimate just how beneficial they may or may not be if run at certain scales.

See also
Q8   What is marginal analysis?
Q20   What is the 'market'?
Q53   How do businesses decide which projects to fund, and which ones to drop?

Q45   What are diminishing returns?

In a production process, as you add more of one productive factor, the extra productivity resulting from each additional unit eventually will become negative: you have reached diminishing returns.

Imagine a production line for frozen pizzas, with people putting toppings on the pizza (sauce, cheese, pepperoni, and so forth) as the base goes past. One person can do only so many pizzas per hour. Adding another person makes the process much more efficient: one person can do the sauce, the other can do everything else. Adding more people makes it even more productive: one person per topping – to a point but, eventually, they will start getting in each other's way, making mistakes, and not increasing the average return to the production of the physical product. Persons four, five, and six represents the start of diminishing returns with respect to labour.

Think about small children and sweets. Feed them one, two, three, four of the sweets, they will get progressively happier (and probably a bit hyper). Give them six, seven, eight sweets, they will probably enjoy these a lot less. By the time you're feeding them sweets 21 and 21, someone has probably called Social Services because of the diminishing returns to their utility the children are experiencing as a result of the increased number of sweets. Don't try this on your own children!

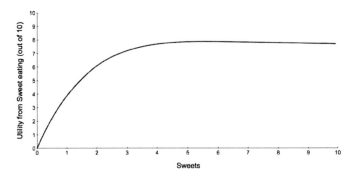

Diminishing returns.

We can graph the extra happiness (or utility) from successive sweets to visualise what is happening to utility. It never drops – a sweet is still preferable to no sweet – but the extra utility the person is getting from the next sweet is vanishingly small after six, seven, or eight of them.

See also
Q41   How does a business decide how much to produce?

MACRO-ECONOMICS

Q46   What are the major '-isms' in economics?

The major '-isms' in economics include:

- Capitalism.
- Socialism.
- Communism.

Capitalism is, essentially, the investment of money – or capital – in the expectation of making a profit. As a system, capitalism rests on the rule of law and the sharp definition of private property between different classes of individuals in society. Capitalism allows people who have the resources to do so to invest time and money in profit-making enterprises. Competition between these enterprises makes each more productive, which increases the output of society, and, eventually, makes everyone better off. Competition within markets creates the competitive pressures that lead to some businesses being winners and others losers. The businesses that win tend to get larger over time, and risk becomes reduced through monopolistic practices. Capitalism is found across most Western economies.

Socialism is a set of concepts based around the notion that society should become more egalitarian over time. While capitalism necessarily generates inequality, because competition generates winners and losers, socialism, by protecting the losers (normally *via* government intervention) tends to agglomerate winners and losers.

Communism is based on the idea that the state should appropriate all property rights centrally, controlling and distributing the work of society from a central point. In this societal architecture, the private business does not work for profit, but rather for society's betterment. True communism has never existed but has assumed different forms as it was tailored to local conditions, and merged with movements for national independence. For example, before the Chinese communists assumed control of the country in 1949, it was clear that their new leader, Mao Zedong (1893–1976), chose to emphasise the continuing role of the peasantry to a much greater extent than his Soviet counterparts. Cuban revolutionary communism is another different form of societal organisation. The basic principles: central command and control of the economy by the state, little or no private property, few private or public freedoms, remain in all forms of communism. Most modern communist states are transitioning from communism to a form of 'managed capitalism' at this time.

See also
Q1   What is economics?

Q47   What is the macro-economy?

The economy can be thought of as a productive engine, as a machine for producing goods and services that people want. It takes raw materials and the factors of production like land, and physical capital, combines them with labour (physical labour and skilled labour) and enterprising, for-profit behaviour, to produce goods and services. These goods and services add to the stock of goods and services already produced in years past, and the economy is said to grow by the amount produced in the economy during the year.

When we discuss the macro-economy, we talk about aggregated variables, which are the sums of individual variables. For example, total private consumption in an economy over a period of time is the sum of all the goods and services consumed in the economy by individual households in a given period, say, a year.

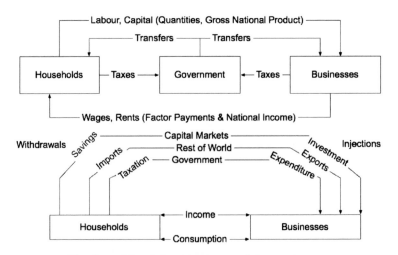

The flow of funds between parts of the economy.

The macro-economy can also be depicted as a flow of funds around the various sectors of the economy. Here the important relationships are between the major agents in the economy: businesses, households, private banks, the central bank, and the government. For a single country, we can represent the flows of funds between the different sectors easily using the diagram above.

See also

Q6   What are the factors of production?
Q27   What is aggregate demand / supply?
Q48   What is an economy's capital stock? Why does it matter?
Q49   How are the parts of the economy connected together?

Q48   What is an economy's capital stock? Why does it matter?

In economics, the capital stock is considered the 'machinery' in a productive process that does not get used up within the process. Consider your kitchen sink, dirty dishes to the right and clean to the left. The water and washing-up liquid are used up, but the sink remains: the products you produce are the clean dishes.

Recently, the definition has been broadened to include:

- Social capital: The value of trust and personal relationships within society.

- Human capital: The value of people's inherent and acquired talent and skills.

- Financial capital: Plain old cash, and obligations.

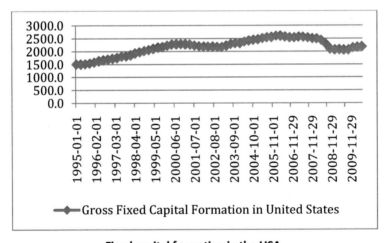

Fixed capital formation in the USA.

Economists measure the capital stock to get a sense of the level of output an economy is capable of at any moment. The capital stock matters, because without it, economies cannot function. Above is a chart of the fixed capital formation of the USA, which reflects the boom-bust trends in the business cycle.

See also
Q47 What is the macro-economy?
Q49 How are the parts of the economy connected together?
Q72 What is the business cycle?

Q49   How are the parts of the economy connected together?

The notion that the economy might be analogous to a circulating system came from a surgeon, François Quesnay, who published a book in 1759 that described cash as blood within an economy, circulating and making the economy wealthier (and healthier), the more of it there was. This is because money can be used on credit to finance transactions and to fund speculation for profit, the whole point of – and instability within – capitalism.

Quesnay's *Tableau Economique* is a depiction of the monetary circuit, showing where money is at any point in time, for the purposes of figuring out at which point it is most efficient to tax it, because that was the most important problem of the day: figuring out where to tax the people to best effect – the economic equivalent of bloodletting.

The circular flow model currently in use (see diagram) depicts the various sectors of society working together, with money and goods flowing between them as workers work for wages, employers pay them those wages, the workers produce the goods which other workers then consume when they go home, and so on.

In the first part of the figure, we see businesses renting capital (for rent) and labour (for a wage) from households. Households then buy the businesses' products and services. The government takes taxes from both households and businesses, and gives back transfers, in the form of subsidies, social welfare payments, government services like healthcare, defence, and education, as well as the legal and peacekeeping activities all governments must perform.

The second part of the figure shows the various 'injections' of cash into the system, and the various withdrawals. Just to take two: when households buy imported goods, cash is withdrawn from the system; similarly, when households save, the cash is withdrawn from the system. However, when saved, the cash goes to the capital markets, which redistribute those savings for profit, so that they go into loans for businesses, which then counts as an injection. International trade means that, while cash is withdrawn from the national system when households buy imports, other households in other countries will buy our country's product(s), and so the nation's businesses will be injected with cash from export markets.

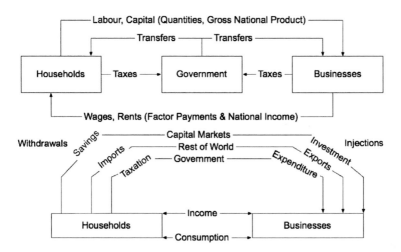

**The circular flow of any macro-economy (above);
the injections and leakages for an open economy (below).**

The circular flow model is the reason national output and income are assumed to be the same thing – your blood pressure is the same, whether measured from the left arm or the right leg. What matters is the pressure and volume of blood being pumped, not the location of measurement. The economy's pulse at any moment is measured by its gross domestic product (GDP).

We use the circular flow model to try to understand why economies sometimes prosper, and why they sometimes fail. The most important aspects of this model is its stress on the interplay of savings and investment in determining the level of national income and output. We see that 'saving' at any moment represents a leakage, and 'investment' an injection. It is very important to remember that different people do different things with their money. Some save, others use those savings for investment. The meaning here of 'investment' is the creation of productive capital, rather than pumping money into something like buying a house or a boat.

The central fact about capitalist economies is that investment is highly volatile from period to period. Investment depends on the amount of savings made in the past, of course, but it also depends on the income of each household and business in the moment of an investment decision. There is no guarantee that savings will equal investment in any period, and so capitalist societies experience 'gluts' of savings, as well as periods where there are none. This is the key reason why economies experience booms and busts.

See also
Q7   What is 'rent'?
Q47   What is the macro-economy?
Q48   What is an economy's capital stock? Why does it matter?
Q70   What is Gross Domestic Product?

Q50   What is inflation?

Inflation is an increase in the general price level. The price level is normally measured using an index called the Consumer Price Index (CPI), which is just one price index. There are many other indices – for example, the wholesale price index, and the producer price index.

The inflation rate is calculated year-to-year (or month-to-month, or even day-to-day) as follows:

Inflation Rate   =   ((Price Index Year 2 less Price Index Year 1) /
                      Price Index Year) * 100.

A price index is calculated by taking a representative basket of goods at any time, and finding out how much they cost, and then returning to the same basket of goods in a few weeks' (or months') time, recalculating the price.

For example, imagine the only thing to be bought in a given moment was 10 loaves of bread, eight bottles of milk, six packets of butter, and one jar of jam. On a given day, a researcher rings around a selection of shops, and asks them how much they charge for the four items. He / she writes down the numbers, waits until the next day, and then rings around again. If the prices have gone up overnight, the price index will go up.

In the table below, the price of jam has stayed the same between Days 1 and 2, but everything else has changed. Bread and butter are both more expensive, while milk is cheaper. Overall, the change in the price index moves the cost of the basket from €24.20 to €37.40. The inflation rate, then, is (37.40 - 24.20) / (24.20) * 100 = 54.5%.

Items in basket	Day 1 €	Day 2 €
Bread (10 loaves)	1	1.20
Milk (8 bottles)	1.15	1.05
Butter (6 packets)	0.50	2.50
Jam (1 jar)	2.00	2.00
Cost of basket	(10*1+8*1.15+6*0.50+1*2) = 24.20	(10*1.20+8*1.05+6*2.50+1*2) = 37.40

How to calculate a price index, and an inflation rate.

This basket of goods is experiencing a very large increase in the price level. Large and persistent increases in the price level like this are called hyperinflations.

See also
Q31   What is an index?
Q51   What is hyperinflation?
Q52   What is deflation and why is it so worrying?

Q51 What is hyperinflation?

Hyperinflation occurs when the price level experiences a very rapid growth, causing the value of money to fall quickly. It is because the value of money falls that the price level increases, as more money is needed to buy the same goods.

Most hyperinflations happen because the government decides to print money, lowering the rate at which money exchanges for goods and services. Hyperinflations also happen during and after wars.

People who live in a country experiencing hyperinflation tend to avoid using the hyper-inflating currency for payment. Instead, they will barter or use another currency (usually dollars) or make very short-term loans to compensate for the uncertainty having such rapidly decreasing purchasing power. Currently, Zimbabwe is experiencing a hyperinflation – the country's currency is essentially worthless.

The notion that the amount of money in circulation determines the price level is called the quantity theory of money. The equation of exchange determines the level of money in the economy:

(1) $M*V = P*T$

where M is the amount of money in circulation, V is the velocity of money (the number of times per year that, on average, a unit of money enters into transactions), P is the price level, and T is the level of transactions.

Originally, the equation involved counting the total transactions within the economy, intermediate as well as final sales, used goods as well as newly-produced goods. Because it is not feasible to get statistics on total transactions, we replace T with Q, the level of gross domestic product, and the concept of P and V are similarly restricted. The equation of exchange becomes:

(2) $M*V = P*Q$

Like any equation, the equation of exchange can be solved for P:

(3) $P = M*V/Q$

We care about how prices change, so we want to represent the equation of exchange in terms of the ratios of the variables at two different times, say, time 1 and time 2. Thus, in this form, the equation of exchange is:

(4) $(P_2 / P_1) = (M_2 / M_1) * (V_2 / V_1) / (Q_2 / Q_1)$

We can use equation (4) to understand hyperinflations. Suppose the amount of money in circulation doubles, so the ratio of Money in time 2 relative to time 1 goes from 1 to 2: $M_2 / M_1 = 2$. The increase in money leads to an increase in the velocity of money of, say, 50% in one year, so $V_2 / V_1 = 1.5$. And suppose the level of economic output drops in the same period by 50% also, so $Q_2 / Q_1 = 0.5$. The ratio of price levels becomes:

(5) $P_2 / P_1 = 2 (1.5) / (0.5) = 6$

Thus, a doubling of the money supply leads not just to a doubling of the price level but to a six-fold increase.

Then suppose the monetary authorities create money to allow the government to cope with higher prices, so the money supply now is increased by six-fold. The velocity of money may triple. The quantity of goods and services in production might drop by another 50%. This would lead to a ratio of price levels of 6 (3) / (0.5) = 36.

An increase in the money supply by a factor of 36 to help cope with this price inflation might lead to an increase in the velocity of money by a factor 10 and, again, suppose the level of output falls by 50%. This would lead to an increase in the price level of 36 (10) / (0.5) = 720. If we keep going like this, it will not take long for the price levels to reach astronomical levels.

The rate inflation in terms of the equation of exchange may be expressed as:

$$\pi = \mu + v - \rho$$

where π is the rate of inflation, μ is the rate of growth of the money supply, v is the rate of growth of the velocity of money and ρ is the rate of growth of real output of the economy.

In hyperinflations in countries with well-established market economies, the level of output does not decrease, but remains constant until the very last stages when the economy really does collapse. For countries making a transition from central control to market-orientation, the output decreases drastically because some state enterprises that are operating at a financial loss have to cut back production drastically, as Russia experienced in the 1990s.

See also
Q50   What is inflation?
Q52   What is deflation and why is it so worrying?
Q70   What is Gross Domestic Product?

Q52   What is deflation and why is it so worrying?

A deflation is a drop in the general price level below zero – that is, the rate of growth of the price index of goods and services drops.

Deflations damage the rate of savings, because they reduce the real value of money over time.

Deflation helps those who are spending today, however, because it increases the real value of money spent today.

Deflation is worrying, because when economies experience deflations at the same time as being highly indebted, they can fall into debt-deflations. A debt-deflation occurs when a fall in the price level raises the real value of nominal debt. This phenomenon can exacerbate the costs of a deflation: households that find themselves heavily in debt do not continue to consume more at the margin, but rather refrain from investing and consuming out of discretionary income in order to pay down loans more quickly.

Consumption by households and investment in productive capacity by businesses, as well as import and export demand, all suffer. The economy contracts as a result of businesses and households trying desperately to pay down their debt, which further deepens the crisis.

Combined with increases in government expenditure from automatic stabilising mechanisms like social welfare payments, the increase in debt-servicing costs can be punitive for small open economies like Ireland, unable to stimulate their economies.

See also
Q50   What is inflation?
Q51   What is hyperinflation?

Q53   How do businesses decide which projects to fund, and which ones to drop?

Cost-benefit analysis is a technique for assessing whether or not to go ahead with a planned course of action. The best example is building a road. One adds up the costs to individuals and to society of building the road, discounting the future effects of the road's construction to today's cashflow.

Discounting is a way of including the benefits and costs the future might bring, while also acknowledging that the future is an unknown country – things may turn out to be radically different. A high discount rate means you are very uncertain about the future; a low discount cost means you are fairly certain of the future.

The process of discounting is easy. Take any process that realises a cashflow. If you gave someone €100, and the interest rate at the time was 5% *per annum*, the person, just by putting the €100 in a bank, could end up with €105 at the end of the first year by adding 5% of €100 to the €100 principal; then 5% of €105 in the second year to get to €110.25, and then €115.76 at the end of the third year.

Look at this the other way around. To make the person who has €100 today indifferent between that amount and some amount in one year's time, you would need to promise the person €105 in one year's time. The old saying 'a bird in the hand is worth two in the bush' comes to mind. Similarly, you would have to give them €115.76 to make them indifferent between €100 today and some amount in three years' time.

Imagine the discount rate is 6%. If a project is forecast to earn €100 in 10 years' time, then that €100, which the project will not earn for 10 more years, is currently worth $100 / (1.06^{10})$, or €55.83.

Returning to our road-building example, the costs of building the road include buying the land, damaging the environment, hiring workers and machinery and buying raw materials, as well as ongoing maintenance. One adds up all the potential benefits: lives saved each year because of the higher quality road, time saved by the number of people who will use the road being able to go faster, and so forth, with all future benefits discounted to the present. Then, compare the costs to the benefits. If the costs exceed the benefits, do not proceed with the building of the road. If the costs are less than the benefits, then proceed with the project.

Although apparently simple, cost / benefit analysis can be a black art. Data is quite difficult to gather on the total cost to society. For example, say migrating birds are affected by the motorway's construction. How are we to value that cost? What about the appropriate choice of discount factor? These are all factors that cloud the interpretation of cost-benefit statistics.

See also
Q41   How does a business decide how much to produce?
Q42   How do businesses know how much to increase prices for a product or service?

Q54   Why does the same amount of money buy less today than when I was a child?

Purchasing power is the amount of a good or service one can command for a given unit of currency. The greater the amount of goods one can buy with, say, €10, the higher the purchasing power of the €10.

In an inflationary period, the purchasing power of currency is diminished, as each €10 buys you less and less goods and services.

In a deflationary period, the purchasing power of a €10 note is increased.

To see this, imagine there is only one good in the world. One day, €10 will buy you 5 units of the good, valued at €2 each. Your purchasing power is 10 / 5 = 2. The next day, due to inflation, €10 will only buy you 3 units, because each good has risen in price. Similarly, the day after, because of a deflation, €10 will buy you 8 units of the good.

See also
Q50   What is inflation?
Q56   Why don't Big Macs cost the same in every country?

Q55   What determines the exchange rate between currencies?

The exchange rate of one currency for another gives the amount of currency A in terms of another (currency B). The exchange rate quoted on the news is generally the spot exchange rate. When you hear the euro trading for 0.93 against the US dollar, it means that $1 will buy you €0.93 worth of goods and services. This is a 'direct' currency quote. If the euro becomes more valuable, or appreciates, then you would expect the exchange rate number to decrease – to say, €0.90, reflecting the fact that $1 now will only buy €0.90 worth of goods and services.

The foreign exchange market is one of the largest by volume in the world, with trillions of US dollars' worth of currency changing hands every day. Only a small proportion of this huge amount now represents actual exchange for business trading purposes, the vast bulk being speculation by banks and investors.

Currencies can be fixed with respect to each other by their exchange rates. Each country in the European Union, for example, has a fixed exchange rate with the euro. Currency can 'peg' to other currencies, meaning the country will maintain a rolling series of fixed exchange rates with respect to one or more other currencies. Most Latin American countries are pegged to the US dollar, for example. Other currencies are free-floating, and have the value of their exchange rates determined by supply and demand for the currency each day. Under floating exchange rates, a currency will become more valuable, or appreciate, relative to other currencies, if demand for it is greater than the available supply. Conversely, if demand for a currency is less than the available supply, the currency will depreciate relative to other currencies.

See also
Q56   Why don't Big Macs cost the same in every country?
Q57   If the government devalues the currency, will this help my business?
Q59   What is an economic and monetary union?

Q56   Why don't Big Macs cost the same in every country?

Purchasing power parity exists when two countries' exchange rates for currency equalise the difference in purchasing power between the two countries.

Think about two currencies, mediated by a flexible exchange rate, which means that, on any given day, the price of euros in terms of dollars changes with the demand for products denominated in the other currency. If we in Europe buy more goods and services from the US relative to their purchases of our goods and services, then the price of that foreign exchange – the exchange rate – will go up.

Now, the higher the price and costs levels are in Europe relative to the US, the greater our imports from the US. High EU prices and low US prices usually means a high price for foreign exchange. The relative change in the exchange rate is in fact proportional to the change in the price levels in the two trading countries. This is purchasing power parity at work, so that, all things being equal, the EU/US exchange rate is given by:

EU / US exchange rate = EU prices / US prices

What has this got to do with Big Macs? If you could buy a Big Mac in Europe for €2 and the exchange rate between the euro and the US dollar was €0.50 for every $1, then if purchasing power parity holds, you should be able to buy a Big Mac in the USA for $1. *The Economist* magazine routinely publishes the prices of Big Macs from all over the world to check for purchasing power parity. The Big Mac is sold in about 120 countries, so the Big Mac purchasing power parity indicator is the exchange rate that would mean hamburgers cost the same in America as abroad, if purchasing power parity held. Comparing actual exchange rates with those implied by the purchasing power parity exchange rate above can help us decide whether a currency is under-valued or over-valued.

It is precisely because currency exchange rates are subject to other pressures, not just purchasing power parity, that sometimes Big Macs do not cost the same in every country.

See also
Q54   Why does the same amount of money buy less today than when I was a child?
Q55   What determines the exchange rate between currencies?

Q57   If the government devalues the currency, will this help my business?

Governments sometimes have control over the exchange rates at which their currencies trade at relative to other countries. It may make sense to decide to devalue the currency in times of economic difficulty. A devaluation is just a downward movement in a country's exchange rate relative to other countries' exchange rates.

If there is a balance of payments deficit, then by devaluing the country makes its imports more expensive (since its currency buys less of other currencies), and its exports cheaper (since other currencies buy more of its goods and services for the same amount of their own currency), thus boosting demand at home and abroad for locally-produced goods.

If the economy is small and open, then the types of goods it imports and exports will be very important, because imports and exports will make up a large proportion of the total goods and services consumed in the economy. Any change in the exchange rate will affect the types of goods and services produced and consumed.

The domestic inflation rate is also very important – an increase in inflation over time could remove all of the gains that a devaluation brings by making locally-produced goods relatively more expensive.

Typically, a country's balance of payments deficit tends to get worse immediately after a currency devaluation, since imports already contracted for and existing debt denominated in foreign currency become more expensive. However, once the prices of imports and exports adjust to the new currency exchange, the effects of the devaluation increase overseas demand for the country's goods, causing the economy to move into a balance of payments surplus. The 'j-curve' shows the lagged effect of monetary policy changes on the real economy, especially with regard to export and import pricing.

So whether a devaluation will help your business depends on whether it is exporting (Yes), importing (No) or producing and selling locally (probably Yes).

See also

Q4   What are economic indicators?
Q50   What is inflation?
Q55   What determines the exchange rate between currencies?

Q58   Why does every country have a central bank? What does it do?

The central bank in any country is its monetary authority. It usually is charged with:

- Implementing monetary policy.
- Ensuring the reserves of the country are accounted for.
- Printing the country's currency.
- Supervising private banks licensed by it to trade within the country.

The central bank is also used as a 'clearing house' for the private banks' transactions and loans.

Finally, if the country has an independent currency, the central bank implements the exchange rate policy of the country.

In Europe, the European Central Bank (ECB) exercises control over the monetary policy of the Eurozone. In particular, the ECB sees its job as promoting price stability throughout the Eurozone.

See also
Q55   What determines the exchange rate between currencies?
Q77   Why does fiscal policy matter?

Q59   What is an economic and monetary union?

Economic and monetary union happens when two or more countries reduce their trade barriers (tariffs on imports) to zero, allow free movement of goods and services as well as capital and labour, and adopt a common regulatory regime and currency – for example, the European Union.

Economic and monetary union is a complex process, demanding a unified set of fiscal and monetary policies.

The benefits of economic and monetary union are lower transactions costs, increased trade, and a strong central bank to maintain low inflation. Among the costs of economic and monetary union are the lack of flexibility it gives member states when dealing with crises, as well as the potential for top-down 'policy straightjackets' that harm regional or national interests. To date, however, the largest economic and monetary union, the European Union, has continued on a slow path of integration between member states – to the betterment of them all.

See also
Q55   What determines the exchange rate between currencies?
Q58   Why does every country have a central bank? What does it do?
Q77   Why does fiscal policy matter?

Q60   Why are cartels banned in most countries?

A cartel is an arrangement between businesses in a sector, which collude to avoid competition with one another. The sellers set common prices, well above their cost bases, to extract maximum consumer surplus from customers. The cartel, jointly, wields market power, which allows them to set up barriers to entry or licensing arrangements, or to reduce product differentiation. Thus cartels turn already imperfect markets into an effective monopoly.

However, in any cartel, there is always an incentive to 'cheat' and to set lower prices to gain increased market share. Thus, stable cartels are rare, although the Organisation of Petroleum Exporting Countries (OPEC), which controls large amounts of the world's supply of oil, is an example of a long-surviving cartel.

Because of their negative effect on competition, and thus on the consumer, the organisation of cartels is illegal in many developed countries.

See also
Q16   What is consumer surplus?
Q17   What is producer surplus?
Q25   What is market structure?
Q26   Why do monopolies matter?

Q61   What is a labour market?

The average person rarely thinks of themselves as an input to productive processes. However, the person's time, their know-how, their muscles, and sometimes their creativity, is combined inside these processes with materials, energy, and the services of capital goods to produce products and services that businesses hope the public will buy. Most people allow this use of their time, skills, and talents because they are compensated for the use of their bodies and minds by a wage or salary.

The labour market is where prospective employers and employees meet. There can be a physical space for a labour market, but most of the time it is a virtual construct: in any sector, there are people who want to work at various wages, and there are people and businesses that want to hire, at different wages. 'Wage' in this context includes all types of compensation arising from work, including non-monetary benefits to the employee like company cars or free lunches at work or extra holidays.

In theory, wages are determined by bargaining between employer and employee, with the employee's age, education, skill level, and ultimately, their productivity, as well as the employer's cost base, being the determinants of the wage they command. Models of the labour market tend to focus on the supply and demand for labour, as in the familiar supply and demand model, or on models where employers and employees search for different and better jobs to fit their preferences. Macroeconomic models focus on the stock of employed and unemployed labour, and their costs and benefits to the economy at any moment.

In reality, things are more complicated. Your socioeconomic status, your parent's professions and incomes, the types of jobs you might hold, the degree of unionisation in them and your social network all play a major role in the probability of workers finding work they will be productive in doing and they all have an influence on the wages paid.

See also
Q2   What is an economic model?

Q7 What is 'rent'?

Q20 What is the 'market'?

Q62   What is the balance of payments?

A country's economic output or income is the sum of consumption, government expenditure, investment, and net exports (exports less imports).

When countries trade with one another, they trade imports and exports for cash.

There are three types of accounts between countries:

- Accounts dealing with goods, services, and income.
- Accounts recording gifts or unilateral transfers.
- Accounts dealing with financial claims, like bank deposits and stocks and bonds.

The first type of account records sales (and purchases) of goods and services from (and to) other countries. For example, if a business in Ireland sells €200,000 worth of goods to a business in China, then that export is recorded in Ireland's current account. Similarly, if the business buys €100,000 worth of goods from another business in Namibia, the import of those goods is recorded in Ireland's current account.

The second type of transaction is someone working in a different country, but sending money home to their family. This transaction is a transfer payment from abroad.

The third type of transaction is a financial one: each year, investors in every country receive billions in interest and dividends from capital investments in foreign stocks and bonds. This account details these transactions.

The balance of payments takes account of these and other transactions.

There are two main parts to the balance of payments system: the current account and the capital account. The balance of payments is the difference between (or the net effect of) the current account and the capital account.

The current account represents the balance of trade between one nation and the rest of the world. When the nation's current account is in surplus, it is earning more from the rest of the world than it is spending.

The capital account records changes of ownership of assets from abroad. The nation's reserves of foreign capital, gold, and other valuable assets are recorded in the capital account.

Countries can generate crises in their balance of payments through excessive borrowing, changing their debt:GDP ratios, or constantly importing rather than exporting goods and services.

See also
Q70   What is Gross Domestic Product?

Q63   What is globalisation?

Globalisation is, mostly, a buzzword. The general idea is that the whole world is being opened up to world capitalism. For economists, globalisation can be defined as the increased interconnection of factor markets (markets for the factors of production).

Today, goods and services are assembled across many countries, with common technologies, common communications, and globalised capital markets. In the case of trade, this has led to global merchandise exports amounting to over 20% of world gross national product in 2007 compared with 8% in 1913 at the end of the last era of globalisation (from 1870 to the start of the First World War).

Various studies suggest that recent globalisation has increased living standards worldwide, but not for everybody: there have been winners and losers from globalisation. All agree that, with reduced transport costs, tariffs and quotas, and the creation of true multinational businesses capable of exploiting changes in demand across the globe, globalisation has changed the international economy in waves that have lasted for centuries. The current wave of globalisation is only the latest in a long series of historical episodes.

See also
Q62   What is the balance of payments?
Q64   Does free trade work?

Q64   Does free trade work?

Yes, if the theory of absolute advantage is right.

In the theory of international trade, absolute advantage is a situation where, when two or more countries trade two or more goods, one of the countries is better at producing both goods. In other words, given two countries, say Australia and Brazil, which can produce two goods, wood and steel, Australia outperforms Brazil in both markets, as shown in the table below.

Country	Output	
	Wood	Steel
Australia	80	80
Brazil	60	70

Example of absolute advantage.

Australia is absolutely more efficient than Brazil in producing both goods. The principle of absolute advantage appears to rule out attempts to make Brazil better off through trade, but the principle of comparative advantage, which superseded absolute advantage, showed it is not the *absolute difference* between each country's costs of production of wood and steel that mattered, but their *relative opportunity costs in production*, which allows Australia and Brazil to specialise in production of either wood or steel.

Thus, although Australia is better at producing both wool and steel, from an opportunity cost point-of-view, it still makes sense for it to trade with Brazil in both commodities.

Therefore there is a role for free trade in helping to increase economic growth internationally.

See also
Q62   What is the balance of payments?

Q63   What is globalisation?

Q65   Why does comparative advantage mean that free trade is almost always better than restricted trade?

Q65 Why does comparative advantage mean that free trade is almost always better than restricted trade?

Comparative advantage is the principle that, through trade in goods, a country can produce a product at a lower cost than another country, still buy from abroad the goods it does not produce at home, and be better off.

Imagine two countries, A and B. They use the same resources to produce two goods, X and Y, in quantities described in the table below. Country B is more efficient at producing both X and Y than country A (an absolute advantage), but still can gain by trade, because it is able to produce X at a lower cost than country A, and let country A produce more Y. Country A has a lower opportunity cost of producing Y, so it should trade X for Y with country B. Both countries benefit.

Country	Output of Good		Opportunity Cost Ratio	
	X	Y	X	Y
A	100	100	1	1
B	180	120	1	2/3 (or 3/2)

An illustration of comparative advantage: why trade can make different countries better off.

See also
Q64 Does free trade work?

Q66   Why do import / export tariffs matter for free trade?

An import tariff is a tax or duty levied on a product when it is imported into a country. Tariffs can be *ad valorem*, specific or compound.

An *ad valorem* tariff adds a percentage increase to the price of the imported product. For example, a 10% tariff on a bicycle worth €100 increases the price of the bicycle in the importing country to €110. *Ad valorem* tariffs are the type most frequently used by the European Union.

A specific tariff is a fixed lump sum levied on an import. For instance, a specific tariff of €5 increases the price of the bicycle to €105. The USA uses both *ad valorem* and specific tariffs.

A compound tariff combines an *ad valorem* and a specific tariff. With a 10% *ad valorem* tariff, and a specific tariff of €5, the price of the imported bicycle rises to €115.

Tariffs matter because they discourage trade, harm the consumer who has to pay higher prices for the goods and services, and give the home-produced good a competitive advantage. There are economic arguments for supporting tariffs – nurturing infant industries, which would collapse under international competition, for example – but the evidence we have shows, on balance, that tariff reductions increase trade, promote competition, increase employment, increase economic growth, and develop living standards.

See also

Q67   What is economic efficiency?

There are many definitions of efficiency used in economics. Most of the time, efficiency in economics refers to the use of available resources to make the highest number (or value) of goods and services from those resources.

There are other definitions, however:

- Social efficiency, where all of society's external costs and benefits are accounted for.

- Allocative efficiency, where a society produces goods and services at minimum cost to consumers.

- Technical efficiency, where the production of goods and services is maximised, using the minimum resources available.

- Productive efficiency, where the production of goods and services is carried out at the lowest factor cost.

Economic efficiency is a desirable quality in any productive process (or economy), because to attain this kind of efficiency means the process is using the fewest units of inputs and the most productive technology to generate its output. Economists would dearly like to find a way to attain economic efficiency (however defined) across the productive processes of society, because it would mean consumers paying the lowest costs for their goods and services, businesses using the best available inputs and producing at the lowest cost, with a high level of benefits to society.

Q68   What are government debts and why do they matter?

Sometimes, it is desirable for a government to spend more than it receives in taxation and profitable trading with the rest of the world. When a government does this, it runs a deficit in its budget. Deficits build up a debt to banks and citizens abroad, and other entities like the World Bank or the International Monetary Fund.

The existence of the debt (especially when it rises rapidly) gives rise to a debate about what terms on which the government should seek to borrow, and what conditions need to be changed through government policy to reduce the rate of growth of the debt, or to increase the rate of growth of the economy as a whole.

Sometimes, a government will adopt expansionary policies that increase aggregate demand and, in so doing, produce the increase in growth the government and society want, while at the same time increasing inflation and decreasing the ability of the government to borrow continually. At other times, the government will adopt austerity measures, where it cuts expenditure on social services and increases taxation in order to reduce the amount it borrows into the future.

In order to borrow, the government must pay interest, and these interest payments transfer income from taxpayers to those who lent the money to the government (usually in the form of government bonds). If the interest rate is very high, then at some point the government must increase the tax burden on its citizens to pay down that debt. The key question is: how can the government borrow and not soak up the liquidity its citizens need to fund their daily lives?

If the government has a Central Bank, the Central Bank can print money at any time to ensure citizens' reserves are always met and kept liquid. But printing money continuously may lead the government straight into a hyperinflation, which is highly undesirable. The Central Bank also can buy securities that already exist (like bonds) on the open financial markets and use the cash generated by the sale to keep the government finances afloat.

Really what has happened is the imposition of a pattern of income transfers between future taxpayers, and those people, institutions, and countries that will hold government securities. This transfer need not be harmful to the poorer people of the country, but it usually is. That is why the national debt matters.

See also
Q50   What is inflation?
Q51   What is hyperinflation?
Q58   Why does every country have a central bank and what does it do?
Q81   What are interest rates and why do they matter?
Q91   Could the government help the economy to recover by reducing taxes?

Q69   What is liquidity?

At any moment, in any economy, there is a stock of money sitting somewhere – usually in a bank and usually controlled by the Central Bank. When I buy something from you, say an apple, for €1, I lose €1, and you gain €1. But the stock of euros is unaffected.

The stock of money in an economy at a given moment is the amount found by adding up the cash in everyone's pockets and the amount they have on deposit (the money owed by banks to their customers), and the amount banks have that they are willing to lend to other customers.

There are lots of different measures of this money stock. One is shown below for the Eurozone. This is called 'm3', and represents the sum of cash in circulation, deposits, and credit available. You can see clearly the percentage change in available cash from 1981 to 2010. There has been a drastic change in the liquidity available in the Eurozone since the beginning of the 2007 crisis.

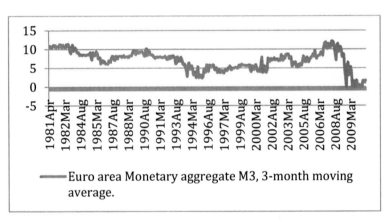

Euro area Monetary aggregate M3, 3-month moving average.

See also
Q58   Why does every country have a central bank? What does it do?
Q78   What is money and why is it useful?
Q79   What is the money supply?

Q70   What is Gross Domestic Product?

Following the Second World War, many countries decided to standardise their national income and product accounts, so they could compare how much each of them had produced in a given year.

The national income and product accounts of any country contain summaries of the amounts consumed, produced, invested, saved, imported, exported, and spent by the government, in a given year. The national income and product accounts also show the flows of funds between the different sectors of the economy. Gross Domestic product is the numerical sum (in today's prices) of the total consumption of goods and services, overall investment, and government expenditure, in that year. Because GDP is measured in today's prices, this measure of GDP is called nominal GDP. To take account of the movement of prices, nominal GDP can be divided by the GDP deflator to give real GDP.

However, GDP is not a measure of overall wellbeing. It is a flawed measure, since it does not take into account resource depletion, environmental destruction, inequality, the black (or grey) economy, or technological change.

One simple example is housework, which is largely unpaid. So, if the numbers of people doing unpaid housework changed, GDP would not change. Similarly, if everyone in the economy were to spend some of their free time cleaning the streets near their homes, GDP would be unmoved, but life would be better, as everyone would have a better environment and would enjoy it a little more. Despite these measurement problems, most policy-makers around the world are obsessed by GDP growth.

Most economists agree that the main way to enrich a country and its people is to create the conditions that allow it to grow its way out of poverty. The determinants of GDP growth are increases in the rate of capital accumulation through savings and investment, increasing rates of technological change, and a steady population growth rate. Because GDP is the sum of all final goods and services produced in the economy in a given year, the GDP growth of an economy can be measured by:

$$GDP\ Growth = ((GDP_t - GDP_{t-1})/GDP_{t-1})* 100.$$

So, for example, if GDP in 2006 was 105, and GDP in 2005 was 100, the growth rate of GDP would be:

$$((GDP_{2006} - GDP_{2005})/GDP_{2005} - 1)*100 = ((105-100)/100-1)*100 = 5\%.$$

See also

Q71   What is the GDP deflator?
Q73   How fast should an economy grow?
Q74   What is economic development?

Q71   What is the GDP deflator?

The Gross Domestic Product (GDP) deflator is a way of accounting for inflation. Related to index numbers, the GDP deflator shows how the cost of different bundles of goods would vary, holding prices constant. It holds base period prices fixed, in contrast to the Consumer Price Index, another measure of inflation, holds base period quantities fixed.

The GDP deflator is calculated by dividing nominal GDP by real GDP, and multiplying by 100. Many countries have their GDP deflators described at this link: http://www.bit.ly/GDPdeflator.

See also
Q50   What is inflation?
Q70   What is Gross Domestic Product?

Q72   What is the business cycle?

The business cycle is the change in growth of the economy over time. The income and output of the economy is measured by Gross Domestic Product (GDP) and Gross National Product (GNP), which is GDP plus imports and minus exports.

The business cycle has several distinct phases:

- Phase 1: Assume the economy has just been through a rough patch, where unemployment rose, and overall demand for the economy's goods and services was depressed for some time. In Phase 1, in the quest for profits, wary businesses keep an eye on two types of prices: the price for receipts, and the price of expenditure. When they see the volume of sales increasing, businesses begin to form expectations that things are getting better. If there is credit available from banks, and businesses see their inventories dropping, they may consider investing for a profit.

- Phase 2: In Phase 2, the economy begins a revival. Banks, in strong lending positions, and perhaps with favourable interest rates as a result of monetary policy, make loans to businesses to expand their productive activities.

- Phase 3: In Phase 3, the economy begins to accumulate stresses. Because there are more jobs, and more demand for all kinds of goods and services, businesses start raising prices. The cost of labour (wages) begins rising as the cost of living rises. The cost of materials rise, eating into profits, and forcing each business to raise its prices, eroding their competitiveness, or eroding their profit margins if they cannot raise prices enough to cover their increased costs. The construction of new plant, new factories, the education of new workforces, all with borrowed funds, leaves businesses (and perhaps governments) in fragile financial positions.

- Phase 4: In Phase 4, at the peak of the cycle, the level of demand for goods and services in the economy is at an all-time high.

Resources like land, capital and labour are being used as fast as possible, and more resources are being imported to service this increased demand. Then something happens. Something unexpected, which leads the people in the economy to realise they are living in a bubble. Very suddenly, errors of optimism lead to a chronic overstocking in certain industries. Rising interest rates, construction and demolition costs, and capital costs, cause a decline in demand for goods and services, and a decline in the demand for labour, resulting in unemployment. People's expectations change overnight, and the economy contracts rapidly through its damaged sectors.

- Phase 5: In Phase 5, the economy is in a recession (defined as two consecutive quarters of negative GDP growth) or perhaps a depression (where the economy contracts for more than four quarters). Prices for goods and services drop, wages drop as a result of unemployment in the damaged sectors, stocks and inventories drop due to sales and fire sales, new processes are developed, and the cycle takes off again.

See also
Q70   What is Gross Domestic Product?

Q73   How fast should an economy grow?

An economy only has a certain amount of capital and labour at any one time. The economy realises its potential output when:

- The resources within the economy, its land, labour, and capital, are being used as efficiently as possible, given the available technology.
- Every worker that wants a job can get one.
- Every piece of investible capital that can be profitably employed is used.

The potential output measure is just a benchmark, to get a sense of how far above or below its potential the economy happens to be at a particular moment.

Most economists believe their economies can grow at between 2% and 4% each year. So, when an economy is in the 'boom' period of the business cycle, GDP or GNP growth may be 10%, implying the economy is above its potential output. Similarly, when an economy is growing at 1%, the economy is operating below its level of potential output, and resources like land, labour, and capital may be underutilised.

See also
Q72   What is the business cycle?

Q74   What is economic development?

Economic development is the process by which agricultural economies are transformed into manufacturing and service-based economies. Since the Industrial Revolution began in the 1870s, countries have followed the same pattern of development, though at different rates.

Economic development is often contrasted with social development, where the development of society as a whole – notably education, health, and fertility – by improving people, and their ability to combine the raw resources they have been given in new and better ways – also is a necessary pre-requisite for growth. It is argued that mere industrialisation (one of the 'stages' of development in many theories), if it comes at the cost of social development, cannot be self-sustaining. Other writers on economic development do not see the process of development as an increase in overall output, but rather a process whereby inequality, unemployment, child mortality, population growth, education, access to medical care, education, and civil rights, are all affected within the process.

Currently, a debate is raging about the efficacy of development aid. Money has been pouring into poorer nations now for decades, with little real change in conditions. Some feel aid is 'dead', and should be stopped. Others feel it should be spent better, and with more oversight. All agree that aid simply does not work as it was intended.

See also
Q33   What is economic geography?

Q75   What is economic inequality?

Economic inequality is defined by the differences in wealth and income between people, and between households. If there are two people in society – you and I – and I am richer than you, then income inequality exists. If I earned less than you last year, but I own much more property or other economic assets, then I may be richer than you overall. Either way, economic inequality exists.

There are many causes of economic inequality – class, gender, labour market decisions, education, ability and talent, and luck are just some of them. Recently, several authors have shown that industrialised, developed societies with less income inequality are happier, more balanced societies.

Named for the statistician Corrado Gini, the Gini coefficient is a measure of income inequality within a group. Gini varies between 0 and 1, with 1 being completely unequal, and 0 being completely equal. Gini is calculated as the mean of the difference between every possible pair of individuals, divided by the mean size. The main aspect of the Gini measure is its ability to compare distributions across different states of the world.

For example, say there are three people in the world. In the first state of the world (A), Andrew has €70, Betty has €20, and Cillian has €10. In the second state of the world (B), Andrew gives some of his money to both Betty and Cillian, equalising income at €33 each. The graph shows that, in state B, the world is more equal, with Gini falling from state A to state B. The Gini coefficient for State A is 0.89, the Gini coefficient for state B, where income has been redistributed is 0.

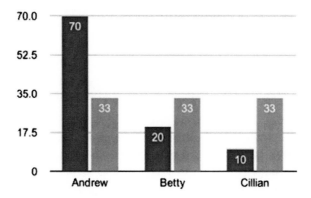

Changes in economic equality, the case of income redistribution.

See also

Q85 What is a poverty trap and how can people get out of one?

Q76   What is the paradox of thrift?

In macro-economics, income in any economy at a point in time is the sum of consumption expenditure and savings. In any year, economic output is the sum of consumption, investment, government expenditure, and net exports.

If everyone in the economy decides to save more than they spend, then the economy's output will collapse, as individual households consume less. The paradox is that increases in savings in the short-run lead to increased investment in the medium- to long-run. But if savings in a period are greater than investment, then there will be a decline in overall output as well.

So while savings are a 'good thing', the old warning about 'too much of a good thing' applies.

ECONOMIC POLICY

Q77   Why does fiscal policy matter?

The word 'fiscal' comes from the Latin *fisca*, meaning purse. Fiscal policy is the use of government funds to change behaviour within the economy.

In 1829, the philosopher and economist John Stuart Mill made the key intellectual leap in understanding how to fight what he called 'general gluts'. Mill determined that excess demand for some particular set of assets in financial markets was mirrored by excess supply of goods and services in product markets, which in turn generated excess supply of workers in labour markets. Mill found that, if one relieved the excess demand for financial assets, one also might cure the excess supply of goods and services (the shortfall of aggregate demand), and the excess supply of labour (mass unemployment). Therefore, there is a role for fiscal policy in stabilising an unstable economy.

For example, say there is an unemployment problem. The government can increase its expenditure this year, and give the unemployed jobs. These new workers will spend their wages on food, clothes, and other wants and desires, and so buoy up the economy. However, the extra government expenditure must be paid for, either by increasing taxes, borrowing, or eating into the country's savings, over time. The fiscal policy mix (sometimes called the fiscal stance) is very important.

The most important component of fiscal policy is the government's budget, which determines how much it will spend on goods and services in a given year. The amount of the budget is usually tied to tax revenues, government borrowing from other countries and other sources of income like printing money, for the government.

In a nation with a neutral fiscal policy, the budget attempts to balance tax receipts and expenditures exactly. Expansionary budgetary policies may create a budget deficit, because the government is spending more than it takes in, at least in the short-term. Contractionary budgetary policies can create a surplus, as tax revenues exceed budget expenditures.

See also
Q23 What are excess supply and excess demand?
Q80 Can the government manage the economy through monetary policy?
Q95 Why is there unemployment and how can it be reduced?

Q78   What is money and why is it useful?

Money is any asset acceptable as a unit of exchange. Paper, gold, rocks, seashells, cigarettes – all can be used as money, as long as one party is willing to exchange their goods for your goods using the money as the unit of exchange. So your goods are valued in terms of the money-units, and so are mine.

The existence of money causes several societal changes. People need not barter any more, avoiding a double coincidence of wants, meaning that I must need what you have and you must need what I have, otherwise neither of us gets what we want. Instead, we each can exchange our goods for money and then spend the money on whatever we want.

The existence of money also causes specialisation in production, reduces the complexity of exchange, and functions as a store of value as well: €10 buys more of the same stuff than €5, all other things being equal.

Money is used as a standard of deferred payment also: I'll give you €10 tomorrow for work done today, and so it allows contracting to take place.

Finally, money is used as a unit of account: we can have €100, €1,000, or €1 million in our bank accounts, and understand what our purchasing power is, in terms of these units.

Money is subject, however, to inflation, deflation, hyperinflation, and disinflation. So be warned: it's not all good.

See also
Q50   What is inflation?
Q51   What is hyperinflation?
Q52   What is deflation and why is it so worrying?
Q79   What is the money supply?

Q79   What is the money supply?

The money supply is the amount of currency in circulation or in use on any given day in an economy. The money supply is important because, if there is too little money in an economy, prices will rise, and economic activity will grind to a halt. If there is too much money supplied to an economy, the value of the money itself collapses, and there may be an inflationary episode, or perhaps a hyperinflation in extreme cases.

There are many measures of the money supply. Some economists look only at the money being used as cash in the system, such as notes and coins. Other definitions include the amount on deposit in banks plus the amount in circulation, plus cash on deposit at private banks, plus cash on deposit at building societies, plus amounts invested in bonds, and so on.

These various measures make up the money supply at any given time. Monetary policy acts on these different measures in different ways, ensuring the practice of monetary policy is an art, rather than a science.

See also
Q50   What is inflation?
Q77   Why does fiscal policy matter?
Q78   What is money and why is it useful?

Q80   Can the government manage the economy through monetary policy?

Monetary policy is a set of tools that governments use to control the levels of spending in an economy. By setting interest rates and reserve rates on levels of funds that banks must have to meet withdrawals, by buying and selling government-backed securities, by deciding how much money to allow into circulation, and by providing credit to private banks, central banks use the instruments of monetary policy to try and keep the economy 'on track'.

So, if the economy is in a slump, central banks can reduce the interest rates at which they lend money to private banks, allowing private banks to lend more cheaply, so increasing the amount of credit in the productive parts of the economy, because banks lend more to more people, and the economy gets stimulated.

If the economy is going 'off track', and inflation is rising as a result, then the central bank can increase interest rates to private banks, making loans more expensive, and ensuring the economy stays 'on track', that is, close to its potential output.

If the central bank wants to reduce the money supply, it can start selling long-dated bonds to the public (usually *via* private banks and lending institutions), which buyers pay for by using their deposits of cash. Banks thus have less money on their books to lend with, and so the volume of lending drops, followed (in theory) by a drop in productive activity in the real economy.

Monetary policy is not a science, but rather an art – and does not always work as intended. In an era of globalised money, the inflows and outflows of currency make operating a domestic monetary policy extremely difficult, even for a large country like the United States. There are many other difficulties besides, including time lags between the setting of monetary policy in a central bank, and its effect on the real world, and the existence of financial 'innovation', where private banks and lending institutions produce 'new' and unregulated financial products, which make the imposition of credit controls very difficult, if not impossible.

See also

Q49 How are the parts of the economy connected together?
Q77 Why does fiscal policy matter?
Q81 What are interest rates and why do they matter?
Q84 Can the government ever really manage the economy?

Q81   What are interest rates and why do they matter?

There are many theories of interest rate determination, but everyone agrees on the definition: an interest rate is a percentage of a principal amount borrowed. The interest rate is the 'price' of borrowing a certain amount at a particular time. When interest rates are high, the 'price' of borrowing is high, and when the interest rate is low, the 'price' of borrowing is lower. There are hundreds, if not thousands, of interest rates for different products at any one time, and yet all behave the same way.

Banks and other financial institutions earn their profits from interest rates, while businesses use interest rates as a signal on whether to begin, expand, or conclude a productive endeavour.

In a loan, the lender normally supplies borrowers with a nominal interest rate, which does not take into account changes in inflation or purchasing power. The real effective interest rate takes account of changes in inflation.

There are many aspects to interest rates: for example, the interest rate can be seen as the price for loanable funds, the degree of one's liquidity preference – the preference for holding money instead of investing it – as well as the degree of risk associated with a particular transaction.

Interest rates matter for everyone who borrows, and everyone who lends, because they set the level of borrowing, and through borrowing, real economic activity that we see in the economy. Think of interest rates as 'levers' that control the activity of the economy. Push the lever up, and the economy will slow down. Pull the lever down, and the economy will speed up, but only up to a point.

When interest rates hit zero, the economy enters a liquidity trap, where the effects of monetary policy are neutralised. Businesses and households will not change their behaviour in response to a change in the interest rate charged by the central bank, because interest rates cannot become negative. There will be no incentive to hold bonds issued by central banks, because they will carry the same interest as cash – zero. That's the trap – the central bank cannot raise interest rates and so dampen down any economic recovery, and it cannot lower them either. This basic plank of monetary policy has failed.

See also

Q82   What is a bank and how does it create money?

A bank is a deposit-taking business that makes money from borrowing and lending.

A loan is a specified amount of money given to a person or a business for a given period of time at a specified rate of interest. For example, my local bank lends me €10,000 at 8% interest for one year. Loans can be secured – backed property or other assets, which get taken by the bank in the event of a default on the loan – or they can be unsecured.

Banks make money, literally, through fractional reserve banking, where only a small portion of deposits given to the bank by its customers are kept in the bank as reserves in the form of cash and other highly liquid assets, which customers can withdraw. The bank lends out the rest of the deposited funds, up to a maximum allowed it by the central bank, while still allowing all deposits to be withdrawn upon demand. The bank can do this because, at any given moment, most people do not attempt to access 100% of their deposits. The rest is loaned out, and when that loan is repaid, the bank gets its principal back, plus interest.

Through fractional reserve banking, banks can create money, adding to the money supply. For example, private commercial banks take deposits from the public. Some of this money they keep, as a reserve to cover withdrawals. Normally, this reserve requirement is set as part of the monetary policy of the central bank of the country. The rest of the money deposited by customers is lent or invested by the bank, to make a profit. The bank thus 'creates' money each time it lends to other businesses and to other banks.

For example, imagine the reserve ratio is 10%, meaning 10% of all a bank's assets must be held to cover withdrawals, and that there are three banks in the world. The first bank receives €100 million worth of money from the public. After setting aside 10% (€10 million) to meet its reserve requirement, Bank 1 lends the remaining 90% (€90 million) to Bank 2, which keeps €9 million on reserve and then lends out the balance of €81 million to Bank 3. Bank 3 again sets aside 10% and then lends on 90% (€72.9 million). In each case, as shown in the table, the bank's assets have been balanced by the level of its liabilities, but there is now more money in the system than when it started. A lot more. In total, with only three banks, there is now €271 million in the system, all brought into being by deposit creation. The process continues for as many banks as there are in the system. Thus, the banking process 'creates' money, literally.

	Bank 1			Bank 2			Bank 3	
	Assets	Liabilities		Assets	Liabilities		Assets	Liabilities
Deposits	100			90			81	
Reserve		10			9			8.1
Loans		90	↗		81	↗		72.9
Total in bank	100	100		90	90		81	81
Total in system	100			190			271	

The fractional reserve system literally 'makes' money by deposit creation.

See also
Q81   What are interest rates and why do they matter?
Q83   How does a government create money?

Q83   How does a government create money?

A government raises funds by three means:

- Taxes.
- Borrowing.
- Printing money.

First, the government can levy taxes on income, on property, on consumption of different goods and services (for example, gasoline and cigarettes, two relatively demand-inelastic products), as well as import and customs duties levied on foreign goods and services, and on sales of capital goods, inheritances, and tariffs.

Taxes can be lump sum – for example, everyone pays €100, regardless of their income – or taxes can be progressive, meaning that tax receipts rise with income, or regressive, meaning taxes fall as income rises. Governments generally raises taxes to fund social expenditures on schools, hospitals, and roads, as well as altering the distribution of income (and hence income inequality) in society. Governments also use taxes to form part of a fiscal policy to stimulate or dampen down the level of total spending.

In addition to taxes, governments can pay for their spending by borrowing from other governments by issuing government-backed bonds. When a government is in fiscal deficit, it must do this to pay for current expenditure.

Finally, governments can raise money by printing money. Money, as we know it today, is *fiat* money – the government simply decides a particular piece of paper is worth €10, the governor of the central bank signs the note, and that piece of paper, which a few seconds ago was practically worthless, is now worth €10. Thus, the government has made a profit by creating money. Government revenue from printing money is called *seigniorage*.

Governments that print too much money run the risk of reducing the purchasing power of each additional note and so, when considering adding to the money supply, they must take inflation, and perhaps the danger of hyperinflation, as well as the economy's position in the business cycle, into account.

See also
Q72   What is the business cycle?
Q82   What is a bank and how does it create money?
Q98   How do taxes impact the market?

Q84   Can the government ever really manage the economy?

In any country, aggregate demand is the sum of consumption expenditure, investment, government spending, and net exports.

During phases of the business cycle when individual households and businesses are cutting back their spending, because of fears about the future, current employment problems, or something else, consumption, investment and / or purchases of imports and exports can fall. This fall in aggregate demand can lead to a vicious cycle, where the economy becomes further depressed because it is depressed. The only agent in the system capable of increasing aggregate demand is the government – by employing workers, beginning large public works programmes, moving or retraining workers, stimulating the economy by changing interest rates to make borrowing cheaper, and even by changing the exchange rate to increase the competitiveness of the country's exports.

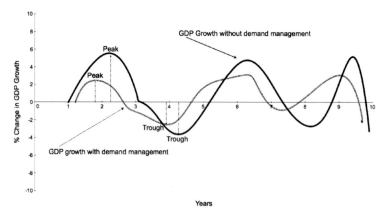

Demand management attenuates peaks and troughs in business cycles.

During phases of the business cycle when the economy is doing very well, the government can change interest rates and government expenditure to decrease aggregate demand, and so attenuate the worst boom and bust moments of the business cycle, achieving a smoothing of the peaks and troughs of the business cycle, as shown in the graph. With active demand management, the peaks are lower, but so are the troughs.

See also
Q80   Can the government manage the economy through monetary policy?

Q85   What is a poverty trap and how can people get out of one?

A poverty trap occurs when the income a person or household might earn from taking a job is less than the combined unemployment benefits they receive while unemployed.

The poverty trap is self-reinforcing because, in the presence of a poverty trap, the longer someone is unemployed, the longer they will remain unemployed.

Poverty traps are serious problems in developing countries, because they can cause economic growth and development to stagnate, and, in countries with large welfare systems, because they damage labour mobility.

There are many ways to reduce poverty traps, including gradation of benefits – reducing benefits the longer a person remains unemployed – or reduction of benefits all together.

Changing tax thresholds for income classes, changing minimum wages, as well as creating tax-credit systems, also can help to alleviate the existence of a poverty trap.

See also
Q75   What is economic inequality?

APPLIED
ECONOMICS

Q86   Is advertising a good thing?

Many people see advertising as the worst product of consumer society. Economically speaking, however, advertising increases market demand for a product by persuading consumers of its advantages over other products. Consumers buy the advertised product in increased volumes, increasing demand. Because of larger market demand, the business producing this product may begin to enjoy economies of scale, which would result in more market output, lower prices, and benefits to consumers.

Rather than stimulating competition, however, heavy (and expensive) advertising of existing brands might make consumers less likely to try new brands, thus raising the cost of entry for newcomers. Thus advertising's role in economic activity is still the subject of much debate.

See also
Q12   Why do economists focus on the consumer?
Q101 How could I spend my money to have the greatest benefit on the economy as a whole?

Q87 How would economists deal with pollution?

An externality is the positive or negative impact that individual decisions have on others besides those specifically involved in the transaction. The best example of a negative externality is pollution. The person who pollutes does not bear the cost of polluting, nor does the person who buys the polluting products. However, those around the polluters – who live near the factories perhaps – bear the cost.

In the presence of externalities, markets tend to fail, meaning they do not price the pollution properly. The private cost to the polluter is not the same as the social cost of polluting activity to society. A tax or subsidy policy normally is applied by economists to bring the marginal cost of pollution – the cost of producing one extra polluting unit – to coincide with the marginal social cost of that pollution.

Similarly, when driving on roads, the problem of congestion happens because an individual car owner does not worry about the effect their driving has on others – they just want to get from A to B. Introducing tolls and congestion charges forces the individual to face the social cost of driving, especially during peak hours, and is an economic solution to the problem of congestion.

Externalities can be positive as well. Infectious disease control, where one sick individual is isolated and treated, thus stopping others from becoming sick, is one example. Another example is art. The artist creates a work of art that is bought, and enjoyed, by one person. If the art is good enough, and survives, the art may be moved into a museum, where many can enjoy it.

See also
Q21 What is market failure?
Q98 How do taxes impact the market?

Q88   What is a demographic transition and will it affect my pension, or hurt my children's chances in life?

As economies develop, the characteristics of their population change as well.

Before industrialisation, birth and death rates are quite high, so the population does not change overly. Countries that industrialise tend to have relatively well-developed medical infrastructures, as well as basic hygiene, safer work and living environments, and nutrition. Their birth rate begins to climb, and their death rate begins to fall. Suddenly a much larger, healthier, population is available for work, increasing income per person in the economy. If income per person is larger than the population growth rate, the economy gets richer and richer. Then, urbanisation, education and labour market opportunities for women begin to reduce birth rates. Small families become the norm. The death rate stays very low, as people stay healthier for longer and live longer. So the population begins to shrink, as fewer children are born per woman to replace those dying. In addition, older people create an economic burden on younger workers, as fewer and fewer workers are available. Following this, a rebound in fertility takes place, as advanced economies are experiencing now. Society replaces itself at a lower rate, following the demographic transition.

Demographic transitions tend to harm the younger members of society, as increased numbers of the elderly in the population must be paid for by younger workers. The more older people there are in a society, the more costly state pensions will be, and the more young workers in an economy, the more intense competition will be over jobs, depressing the wage rates younger workers will see.

See also
Q72   What is the business cycle?

Q89   Can an individual ever beat the market?

The efficient markets hypothesis is a largely discredited theory purporting to explain why the financial markets are very hard to beat. The basic insight is that the market price of any item (stock, bond, commodity) always reflects available information about it.

There is a joke between economists, about an economist strolling down the street with his son. They come upon a €10 note on the ground and, as his son reaches down to pick it up, the economist says, "Don't bother – if it were a genuine €10 note, someone would have already picked it up". This story tells you everything you need to know about the efficient markets hypothesis.

If a market is 'efficient', then it reflects all available information about assets for sale in the market. Take Apple computers, for example. Were the CEO of a major company to be hit by a meteor on the way to work and die, the news of his / her demise would cause the price of their company's stock to plummet, as worried investors would sell off the stock, bidding down the price. This is the market reacting to new information by changing the price of stocks. The insight of the efficient markets hypothesis is that, in an informationally-efficient market, price changes must be unforecastable if they are properly anticipated, that is, if they fully incorporate the information and expectations of all market participants.

In the strongest version of the hypothesis, the market has full public and private information – including the CEO's risk attitudes, his medical history, all available star charts, and so on. Weaker versions concentrate on 'event' analyses, like a CEO being hit by a meteor. The behaviour of everyone in the market makes the market price look completely random – it will not be possible to predict tomorrow's stock movements from today's prices if the market is efficient in this sense. There will be no trend to plot, because there will be no undiscovered information. All available information will be priced in already by the profit-seeking activities of market participants. And thus the market will be impossible to beat.

See also

Q20   What is the 'market'?

Q90   Should we tax more or less?

The Laffer curve is the only truly falsified empirical prediction in economics. Arthur Laffer predicted that the relationship between tax rates and overall levels of taxation revenue is parabolic. That is, at low levels of taxation, increasing the tax rate slightly will result in large increases in taxation revenue, because you are travelling up the curve, as shown in the diagram below.

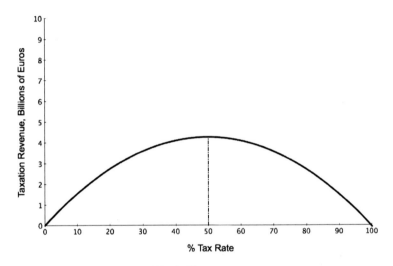

The Laffer curve.

At higher levels of taxation, increasing taxation rates makes no sense, because the increase in taxation revenue gets smaller each time, and exerts a negative effect on incentives to work, as well as to declare income for tax. There is a feedback effect at work as well: if the theory works, tax cuts can generate more tax revenue for the government because it changes people's behaviour, increasing the level of economic activity, which creates more taxable income, and the economy grows faster—this is a virtuous cycle.

Governments tried to follow the logic of reducing taxes, in order to increase incentives to work, increase income, and spend more in the economy. The logic failed utterly.

Should we tax more or less? When the feedback from increasing the topmost rate of tax actually decreases the amount of taxation revenue collected, it is time to lower taxes. In the vast majority of cases, most economies find themselves on the left hand side of the curve. This means that most taxation increases do increase the amount of money governments collect—so tax cuts don't usually pay for themselves. Nonetheless we should tax less if we can, as high taxes function as a disincentive to honest work.

See also
Q91 Could the government help the economy to recover by reducing taxes?

Q98 How do taxes impact the market?

Q91   Could the government help the economy to recover by reducing taxes?

In a recession, tax cuts can improve the economy's output by giving people more purchasing power and higher consumer confidence, which leads to them spending more of their incomes on goods and services. This increase in demand for goods and services leads to more jobs, more business confidence, which leads to more business investment in more efficient technologies, and ultimately higher GDP growth, after the increased spending by consumers filters through the rest of the economy. Tax cuts can be part of a *laissez faire* economic policy, where the policy-makers believe the economy and the markets that make up the economy should be freed from government interference.

Lower taxes, when coupled with lower or controlled government spending, can help the economy. Because the government collects taxes from several sources – income, consumption, and so on – it increases its revenue in other categories of government taxation, because, again, the tax cut encourages people to buy more products and services, stimulating the economy and creating more jobs.

Lower taxes (as a percentage of income) going to the government coffers and more staying in the pockets of average taxpayers may have a positive effect on the overall economy and allows a vibrant free democracy to thrive and grow in the short term; however, the provision of government services will suffer as a direct result.

The key question is the offsetting effects of lower taxation: lower taxes on manufacturing, service and business sectors allows these sectors to spend more money on their businesses and to create more jobs, which increases spending again. If the job creation from increased investment delivers more revenue through taxes as a result of this increased commercial activity and thus allows the government to maintain, or even increase, spending on social programmes, the tax cut is clearly a good idea. The resulting increased revenue allows a responsible government to borrow less money or even to reduce government debt, relieving pressure on currency supply and interest rates, resulting in lower interest rates, which is good for everyone. In the 'rose-tinted' version of this story, lower tax rates are a classic case of 'less is more' and any good government should always be searching for ways to reduce taxes and spending.

However, this 'rose-tinted' version of the story ignores the unequal distribution of income. If taxes are cut as a percentage of income, then those who earn the most have the most to benefit from the tax cut.

Imagine there are two people in the economy, Alfred and Bob. Alfred earns €100 a week, while Bob earns €10. If taxes are cut from 10% to 5%, then Alfred saves €5, but Bob only saves €0.50 in the tax change. If the cost of government services to Alfred and Bob is, say, €7, then the services will have to be pared back because there is now only €5.50 in taxes to pay for the services. Who will suffer from the reduction of services? Bob will, because Alfred has the spare cash to afford his own services. However, if Alfred buys those services from Bob using his extra €5 in disposable income, then the tax reduction helps everyone. If Alfred does not spend his newly-acquired €5 in this way, then Bob clearly loses out. When the benefits of a tax cut do not extend to all social classes, or the benefits disappear after a short time, then a tax cut may be a bad idea, especially if the taxes pay for needed public services.

See also

Q15   Why are expectations important?
Q21   What is market failure?
Q90   Should we tax more or less?
Q98   How do taxes impact the market?

Q92   Could we ever have a zero inflation economy?

Yes, with perfect information about the economy, and a very good control over the money supply in the economy, but there would be serious consequences to having no inflation, as opposed to deflation or inflation, in the economy.

Remember that an inflation is a general rise in the price level. If there is no inflation, then consumers will be very happy, because they can purchase more goods and services with the money they have. Producers of goods and services will not be too happy, however. Producers will not be able to receive more money for their goods and services, meaning their profits will not go up. There will be little incentive to invest in improving the quality of the goods and services they produce, which would create more jobs, and grow the economy.

Price changes are like signals in the economy, which consumers and producers react to. Having a zero inflation economy would be like turning those signals off. Most economists would be very happy if we could guarantee 2% or 3% inflation in an economy each year.

See also
Q50   What is inflation?
Q80   Can the government manage the economy through monetary policy?

Q93 Why does increased productivity matter for an economy?

Productivity growth – gains in the efficiency with which capital, labour and technology are used in an economy – is the elusive holy grail of economic development.

When economists say that productivity growth is the root cause of development, they almost are stating a truism. For example, from the late 1970s to the early 2000s, Latin America suffered a macroeconomic slump, accompanied by high inflation and the destruction of credit. Political instability – and expropriations of businesses – in some countries also discouraged businesses from growing. It is hardly surprising that productivity suffered but, once productivity begins to rise, it compounds, making further gains more probable, and enriching each country.

Progress in productivity means an increased standard of living for everyone in the economy. In the long run, real hourly earnings are tied to productivity gains. A more productive economy is able to produce more goods and services, not by increasing resources such as labour, but by making production more efficient.

Productivity growth also helps offset inflation and encourages economic growth by better allocating resources and improving the effectiveness and efficiency of human capital.

See also
Q74 What is economic development?

Q94   Why does everyone want to buy a house?

For most people, buying a house is the largest single investment they will make in their lives. They borrow, normally, for the duration of their working lives to buy a house. If they buy at the wrong moment, the chances of this purchase ruining them are very high. So why does everyone want to buy a house?

Considered in purely economic terms, a house (or any property) is just an asset, like a stock or a bond or a block of gold. Unlike these asset classes, of course, you might live within the house. The confusion between the use value of a house – as shelter – and the exchange value of the house – as asset – causes more booms and busts within advanced economies than any other type of asset boom or bust.

When house prices rise, consumer confidence rises. Consumers think they understand house price changes. They attribute these changes to changes in demographics, increased economic integration, post-war rebuilding, national destiny, deregulation, or something else. Everyone searches for proximate causes for the house price boom, but the cause is secondary to an estimation of how long the boom might actually last. People increase their spending and their borrowing during the housing boom, confident that they are sitting on (sometimes literally) an asset whose value is rising sharply. Homeowners go into debt to buy the house itself, convinced that rent is 'dead money'. Homeowners can borrow against the rising value of the house's equity as well, in a process of mortgage equity withdrawal.

Now, once the boom inevitably turns to bust, the falling price of housing damages consumer confidence and investment in every other part of the economy, and people whose houses are worth less than the value of their mortgage loan enter negative equity. The more people in negative equity, the more damaged the economy has become by the scale of the housing boom and bust cycle.

There is a long history of bubbles blowing up and bursting in housing, yet there is a popular perception that there is no more reliable investment than housing. Since 1975, for example, house prices in the United Kingdom increased on average by 3%, when you take away the effects of inflation. But the average hides huge swings in prices over the 30-year period.

The price of any house is a combination of the cost of the land that the house stands on, the materials and labour that went into the construction of the house, the regulations governing the building itself, and the mark-up attached by the builder to the house's construction. The price of land can change quickly, which changes the underlying value of the house. In addition to the 'fundamental' value of the house like the supply and demand for housing in a particular area, the expectation of house price increases also changes rapidly, and it is this expectational component that causes the quick price changes within the housing market.

Historically, up until the First World War, very few homes in countries like the UK were owner-occupied; only 1 in 10 houses in the UK in 1914 were owner-occupied. This was, in part, because property titles rested with richer elements of UK society, who made money by renting. Through tax reliefs for home buyers and construction subsidy schemes for sellers, successive governments have succeeded in expanding the number of owner-occupiers across the developed world. Today, for example, 85% of people in Spain are owner-occupiers, 77% of people in Ireland, 69% in the UK, but only 42% of Germans own their own homes.

The fact that such a large part of society owns property actually retards the normal market impulses, where prices rise and fall to their natural levels. The existence of a politically-contentious issue like home ownership and price supports increases the likelihood of bubbles forming.

See also

Q15   Why are expectations important?
Q72   What is the business cycle?
Q100   Why does a change in central bank lending rates affect my mortgage?

Q95 Why is there unemployment and how can it be reduced?

Unemployment is present in every society. Normal people tend to think about unemployment in terms of people who want to get a job who cannot get one. Economists tend to think of unemployment in terms of factors of production being underutilised. The elimination of unemployment is one of the goals of macro-economics.

The unemployment rate is the number of people defined as unemployed divided by the number in the labour force. Most of the time, unemployment is measured by a population survey. Regardless of which survey method is employed, there are always people who are unemployed, and resources (land, factories, inventories) similarly underused. Macroeconomic theory suggests that unemployment occurs when there is not enough demand for goods and services within the economic system. Therefore, there is a role for fiscal policy in purchasing goods and services in times of unemployment (troughs in business cycles) to encourage unemployment to fall.

There are three routes to reducing unemployment.

First, emigration. When workers leave for better things, this will reduce unemployment. Emigration is not, of itself, a bad thing. Workers can make a better life for themselves abroad than they would have made at home, and can contribute both to the new economy they live in, and also to their home countries by sending money home. Migrant workers can also return home after some time, bringing with them the skills they have learned abroad, and adding to the wages they can command (and their corresponding lifestyles) as well as enriching society.

The second route to reducing unemployment is job creation by the public sector. This is where the government or government agencies hire more people to do various things like sweeping roads, building buildings, teaching economics, and so forth. This is the state functioning as the employer of last resort.

Third, the private sector creates jobs. This is the best type of job creation, as it does not cost the taxpayer anything to produce these jobs, and the jobs are generally in productive areas where there is a market demand. The government can help to spur private sector job creation by making it cheaper to hire someone, by reducing employer taxes, by making it easier to find the right person using skills-matching databases, by paying for individuals to train themselves into being the right person for the job by (re-)educating them, or simply by creating a range of government services that require private sector input—green technology, say—and focusing on these.

When the economy experiences a slump, and large numbers of workers are made unemployed, the government needs to be throwing huge resources at individuals willing to take a risk, to set up a new small businesses, in the hopes that some of these companies will succeed. The government also needs to court more businesses from abroad as foreign direct investment.

See also
Q61   What is a labour market?
Q77   Why does fiscal policy matter?
Q80   Can the government manage the economy through monetary policy?

Q96   What is the trickle-down theory?

More a caricature of another theory than a real theory in its own right, the trickle-down theory holds that decreasing taxes, or increasing subsidies and grants, to businesses and wealthy households will result in a 'trickle-down' effect, whereby their increased spending, because their disposable incomes have increased, will lead to an indirect benefit for those who did not receive the subsidy. The eminent economist JK Galbraith defined it as "the less than elegant metaphor that, if one feeds the horse enough oats, some will pass through to the road for the sparrows".

Similarly, those who benefit indirectly will benefit even more if businesses and the wealthy get tax decreases and helpful subsidies. This feedback effect is supposed to help the economy recover.

Trickle-down theory is often identified strongly with supply-side economics, and with Say's Law. Jean Baptise Say (1767-1832) held that supply creates its own demand, because income must be spent in some fashion. If Say's law holds, then the best way to ensure markets work well is to allow them to function without regulatory oversight, or without government interference. The central idea of supply-side economics is based on Say's Law: let the market price vary to find its clearing quantity. If everyone in society was working, then every household would decide how much of their incomes to save or consume. In the simplest version of Say's story, this implies investment must adjust to meet all the available saving. The accumulation of physical capital – the measurement of economic development – is driven by changes in productivity, and changes in saving behaviour.

See also
Q20   What is the 'market'?
Q74   What is economic development?

Q97 How do organisations like the World Trade Organisation influence world trade?

The World Trade Organisation (WTO) and its predecessor, the General Agreement on Tariffs and Trade (GATT), influence world trade by providing a forum where countries can agree to reduce bi-laterally or multi-laterally the tariffs and quotas they charge for importing each other's goods. The WTO helps to regulate the terms on which nations exchange goods and services.

Under the GATT, countries met periodically for 'rounds' of negotiations on lowering trade restrictions between countries. Each round is named for the place it is held, so the 'Uruguay' round in 1986 took place in Uruguay. The WTO is really an expanded version of the GATT, and was established in 1995. The main thrust of each round of negotiations is the removal of export subsidies, import tariffs, and dumping.

Export subsidies exist when a government provides support such as subsidies, tax breaks, or direct state aid to private firms or industries. This is unfair, as it means firms in other countries will find it harder to compete with a firm getting an export subsidy or tax break.

Import restrictions come in many forms, the most common are import quotas and tariffs. Tariffs are taxes on imports. They may take the form of simple percentages, where a car imported from the USA to the UK must pay a 15% (say) tax to the government, increasing its price relative to UK cars and decreasing demand for them. Import quotas function in much the same way. By restricting the supply of cars to a certain number in a year, say, import quotas ensure the price of the US cars will be higher (as supply is restricted), and make it harder for a foreign competitor to make money.

Anti-dumping legislation is important to safeguard home producers of goods and services. Say the EU's production of corn is cheaper, because of increased technological efficiency, and because of subsidies received from the European Union's Common Agricultural Policy. If there is an overproduction of corn in one year, the EU might decide to flood the corn markets of Africa with corn that is cheaper than the corn produced locally, harming local businesses in the importing country.

Finally, the WTO is instrumental in setting up regional customs unions and free trade agreements, where groups of countries voluntarily agree to remove or reduce trade barriers between themselves. The original European Coal and Steel Federation, begun in 1948, which allowed France and Germany to trade in coal and steel at preferential rates, is an early example of such an agreement.

See also
Q63 What is globalisation?
Q64 Does free trade work?
Q66 Why do import / export tariffs matter for free trade?

Q98   How do taxes impact the market?

Taxation is a large part of the role of government in society. Taxes come in many forms and perform many functions. Taxation policy is sometimes carried out to disincentivise behaviours – for example, taxes on cigarettes to prevent adverse health care outcomes from smoking. Taxation policy is used sometimes to redistribute income from those with jobs, to those without. So employees are taxed while they work, to pay for those who do not work. Employees often contribute towards health and pensions policies through their incomes, which is a means of redistributing income from the present to the future. Sometimes, taxes are levied on property values, or on the sales of properties. And capital gains taxes affect the sales of large capital goods like businesses, buildings, and houses.

Overall, taxes of any shape serve to *distort* the market. I do not mean this is in a pejorative sense, only that taxes can and will affect the shape and composition of the market, distorting the 'true' price somewhat. Take a look at the diagram below.

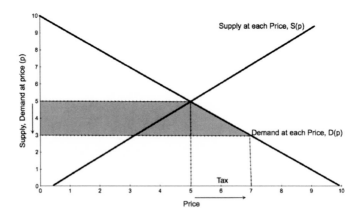

The effect of tax on a market.

We see a market for goods in supply and demand equilibrium at 5 units bought and 5 units sold for a price of €5 each. Now let us impose a tax of

€2 per unit on the market, meaning that every time a good is bought, the supplier must add a sales tax to the price of the good, driving the price from €5 to €7. We can clearly see the distortion. Some of those consumers who would have purchased the good do not do so, because they are priced out of the market. Suppliers lose out as well, through goods never produced, sometimes called a 'deadweight loss'.

See also

Q99   How do reductions in Government spending affect the economy?

The government is the largest business in most countries. It hires the most people, buys the most cement, builds the most buildings, and keeps more businesses going with demands for services than any other entity. When governments decide to rein in spending, there are several effects.

First, if everything else in the economy is kept constant – consumption, investment, exports, and imports – then the level of economic output will fall. Second, because the government hires and keeps many of the nation's citizens alive, increased unemployment and decreased consumption *via* reductions in disposable income reduce overall levels of spending in the economy, which collapses the confidence of investors, causing investment to decline as well. The economy contracts by more than the cuts the government will make, because of the size of the government in relation to the economy as a whole, and because of the deeply intertwined nature of the government as a supplier and demander of goods and services with the rest of the economy.

See also
Q10   What is utility?
Q20   What is the 'market'?
Q94   Why does everyone want to buy a house?

Q100   Why does a change in central bank lending rates affect my mortgage?

Central banks are called the 'lender of last resort', meaning they will always supply liquidity to the economic system, even when banks are bust. Private banks (the ones that lend mortgages to households) borrow from discount houses, which act as a sort of buffer between them and the central bank. Discount houses buy short-dated government bonds, bills of exchange, and Treasury bills, all of which are promises to pay a stated sum by a stated date sometime in the future. Discount houses buy these financial instruments for a price less than face value (the promised payment); the difference between what the discount house pays and what the face value provides the discount house with its income. The discount house borrows day-to-day from private banks. When private banks find they are lending close to the legal limit of their reserves, they refuse to renew part of their loans to discount houses, and the discount houses then must access the 'Bank Rate' set by the central bank.

This 'bank rate' is set by the head of the central bank. By reducing private banks' cash in hand and at the central bank by selling securities on the open market, the central bank can force private banks to cut down their loans to the discount houses. This roundabout transaction means the government (or the central bank, if it is independent) can set the short-term borrowing rate for private banks.

Private banks issue mortgages for homes and businesses. When the central bank increases its 'bank rate', private banks pass on their increased cost of acquiring capital to you, the mortgage holder, *via* the discount houses. So you see your monthly mortgage payment rising as a result.

See also

Q58   Why does every country have a central bank? What does it do?
Q81   What are interest rates and why do they matter?
Q94   Why does everyone want to buy a house?

Q101 How could I spend my money to have the greatest benefit on the economy as a whole?

And a bonus question-and-answer!

The beauty of economics is that, by each of us pursuing our own best interests, the market system arrives at an allocation of goods and services that is as good as, if not better than, any other allocation mechanism. The best way to spend your money is to make sure you are not directly harming anyone by doing so, and then to try and spend the most you can, while making sure your future needs as you perceive them right now are covered. So, savings become important, pensions and healthcare become important, rainy day money becomes important.

It will not matter whether you spend your money on goods produced in your home country, or goods produced in other countries, though it might seem like spending money on domestic goods keeps money inside the economy; however, if those goods are more costly than goods produced abroad, by reducing your disposable income, you are harming yourself and the economy. The case of Taiwan is instructive.

Taiwan is an interesting case study in economic management. Taiwan's growth strategy is export-led, with the main drivers of Taiwanese growth being electronics, and electronics-related industries. Taiwan was a 'Tiger economy', in that it industrialised and developed quickly after the 1970s. Taiwan was badly hit by the Great Recession of 2007--2010. In the middle of 2009, Taiwanese officials were forecasting a drop in GNP of around 8%. In 2009, however, Taiwanese real GDP fell year on year by only 1.87% as a result of a downturn in exports. Taiwan experienced a deflation in 2009, but it was running a huge current account surplus, as it almost always has, so small scale and large scale stimulus programmes were going to be possible when a downturn came.

Here's one: Taiwan introduced a voucher system in early 2009 in response to the downturn. The voucher was for around €75, and allowed millions of Taiwanese people the chance to increase their domestic consumption over the period of the downturn. No doubt this measure kept many businesses afloat during the period, and kept expectations from falling lower than they might have otherwise. A large current account surplus, a counter-cyclical fiscal policy, simple expansions of public works schemes and textbook Keynesian demand stimuli, coupled with the export-led recovery buoyed by other economies' stimulus programmes (notably China and the US, Taiwan's two biggest trade partners), and a demonstrable lack of a housing bubble, mean that the Taiwanese were back in the black after 9 months.

See also
Q72   What is the business cycle?
Q84   Can the government ever really manage the economy?

ABOUT THE AUTHOR

Stephen Kinsella is a lecturer in economics at the University of Limerick, Ireland. He is the author of Ireland in *2050: How We Will be Living*, Liberties Press, 2009; editor (with Tony Leddin) of *Understanding Ireland's Economic Crisis*, Blackhall Publishing, 2010, and co-editor of *The Elgar Companion to Computable Economics*, Edward Elgar, 2010. He holds a BA (Mod) from Trinity College, Dublin, in economics, an MEconSc and PhD from NUI, Galway, and an MA, MPhil, and PhD from the New School for Social Research, New York, all in economics. He is interested in computable economics, experimental economics, and Irish public policy.

ABOUT THE QUICK WIN SERIES

The **Quick Win** series of books, apps and websites is designed for the modern, busy reader, who wants to learn enough to complete the immediate task at hand, but needs to see the information in context.

Topics published to date include:

- QUICK WIN MARKETING.
- QUICK WIN DIGITAL MARKETING.
- QUICK WIN B2B SALES.
- QUICK WIN LEADERSHIP.
- QUICK WIN MEDIA LAW IRELAND.
- QUICK WIN SAFETY MANAGEMENT.

Topics planned for 2011 include:

- QUICK WIN LEAN BUSINESS.
- QUICK WIN SMALL BUSINESS.

For more information, see **www.oaktreepress.com**.

QuickWin

MARKETING

Answers to your top 100 Marketing Questions

Annmarie Hanlon

Lightning Source UK Ltd.
Milton Keynes UK

175997UK00001B/68/P